Public Transportation:
On the Move...

Edited by
Marc Wortman, PhD

Consulting Editor
John Morris Dixon, FAIA

Designed by
Harish K. Patel

Visual Reference Publications, New York

The American Public Transportation Association, Washington, DC

Visual Reference Publications Inc.
302 Fifth Avenue
New York, NY 10001

Distributors to the trade in the United States and Canada
Watson-Guptill
770 Broadway
New York, NY 10003

Distributors outside the United States and Canada
HarperCollins International
10 East 53rd Street
New York, NY 10022-5299

Library of Congress Cataloging in Publication Data:
Public Transportation: *On the Move*

Printed in China
ISBN 1-58471-037-3

Contents

American Public Transportation: Toward a Comprehensive System

America's continuing love affair with the car has many benefits that most of us enjoy. However, those benefits have also come at a substantial and increasing price. That price has been traffic congestion with its enormous social burdens of wasted time and energy, along with environmental degradation and pollution, development sprawl and loss of open space, urban disinvestment, unhealthy sedentary lifestyles and reliance upon foreign energy sources.

Regionally and nationally these reasons have helped to spur a renewal in the use of and investment in public transportation. Public transportation represents a sensible, cost-effective, environmentally sound alternative to driving ourselves. However, as communities develop transportation alternatives, they cannot deny the continued value and importance of the car; instead, any effective public transportation mode should go hand-in-hand with the existing street and highway network to forge a comprehensive transportation system that, at its best, incorporates the full range of travel modes. Developing such a comprehensive, integrated and interconnected system—locally, regionally and nationally—requires thoughtful planning and imaginative design, application of advanced technologies, careful assessment of existing and future public needs and significant public investment in multi-modal infrastructure. An integrated, comprehensive, far-sighted approach will be critical if communities are to remain economically competitive.

The promise contained in today's public transportation renaissance—for which many of the firms represented in this book are responsible—will only be achieved if each new element serves to weave together the existing transportation networks and leaves open the possibility for future growth.

Public investment in transit systems has increased substantially in recent years, especially in fast-growth metropolitan areas of the South and West where the car has long dominated. Many people living in those parts of the country now recognize that their growth cannot be sustained once their communities begin to choke on their own congestion and unplanned sprawl. Cars and public transit need to be integrated into a coordinated transportation system, while future growth gets channeled along planned transit corridors.

With scant tradition for either transportation planning or public investment in many parts of the nation, building support for public transportation requires a community-wide effort. The success of new and enhanced public transportation systems in metropolitan areas where the car has long been king—places represented in this book like Atlanta, Dallas, Salt Lake City, Phoenix,

Los Angeles, Seattle and Denver—proves it is possible. Boston, New York, Chicago, Washington and many other cities with aging public transportation infrastructure have been making major upgrades in their already highly respected systems. Other communities have come to recognize that America's most successful civic cultures embrace public transportation as full partners within their transportation infrastructure.

The achievement and the potential in public transportation come through in every page of this survey. This book clearly shows an efficient, well-run, safe and effective public transportation system boosts the economy, enhances quality of life and quickly becomes a source of civic pride. The designers, builders and consultants whose work is displayed here have much to boast about already. Transportation systems are highly technical endeavors, especially in an age in which technology enables many of the most valued advances. However, as project after project depicted here shows, successful public transportation systems only emerge where the public in public transportation gets emphasized. That is the only way to keep *public* transportation in America on the move.

—Marc Wortman, PhD

Contents by Type of Project / Vehicle

Note: Many projects are of more than one type and therefore may be listed under more than one category.

Preface

William W. Millar
President
American Public
Transportation Association

The American Public Transportation Association (APTA) is pleased to sponsor Public Transportation: On the Move, highlighting the renaissance of public transportation and showcasing state-of-the-art projects and vehicles.

Throughout North America, public transportation is experiencing a rebirth. Steady increases in investment have dramatically improved and expanded public transportation services and attracted record numbers of riders on modern systems in urban, suburban and rural areas.

APTA's 1,500 members have been instrumental in paving the way for a revival of the public transportation industry by launching new services, embracing innovation and improving customer service.

Public transportation is synonymous with opportunity and choices for Americans from all walks of life. Public transportation benefits every segment of society through improved mobility and economic development. It reduces congestion, improves our air and helps address the needs of a growing and changing population.

These numerous benefits of public transportation make a powerful case for continued investment in the nation's transportation network today to ensure it keeps pace with tomorrow's increasing demands.

While the public transportation industry has made great progress in the last decade, there are plenty of challenges still ahead. In small cities and rural areas, two-thirds of all residents have few, if any options. The solution will require more investment and coordination among federal, state and local governments.

The projects and businesses presented in this book are just a sampling of the public transportation industry's accomplishments in recent years. As we build on these advancements, it is clear the best is yet to come.

About APTA

APTA is a nonprofit international association of 1,500 member organizations including public transportation systems; planning, design, construction and finance firms; product and service providers; academic institutions; and state associations and departments of transportation. APTA members serve the public interest by providing safe, efficient and economical public transportation services and products. APTA members serve more than 90 percent of persons using public transportation in the United States and Canada.

Public Transportation: Moving Forward

The Renaissance

Public transportation is moving in the right direction. From small towns to big cities, a renaissance in public transportation is helping bring vitality to communities.

America's public transportation systems are experiencing record high levels of customers. Since 1995, public transportation ridership has grown 21 percent, which is faster than the growth rate of the population of the United States as a whole. Indeed, it is also greater than the rate of increase in domestic air travel and highway use during the same period of time. Today, over 14 million Americans board public transportation each day, taking 9.4 billion trips annually.

Americans rely on public transportation to take them to work, to shop, to the doctor and to visit family and friends. Transit systems have even become sources of civic pride and the hottest ticket in town in many areas. Local systems are partnering with community groups for holiday events, fairs, festivals and sporting events. Utah Transit Authority's TRAX light rail system, attracting over 40 percent more riders than originally projected, played a key role in moving the thousands of spectators attending the 2002 Olympic Winter Games. Sports fans in Baltimore, Cleveland, Denver, San Diego and other cities are finding games more enjoyable when they can take public transportation and do not have to deal with traffic jams and parking hassles.

Communities across the country are seeing growth in all modes of public transportation. Currently, in metropolitan areas, there are 14 heavy rail systems, while the number of commuter rail systems has doubled to 16 since 1970. Since 1980, the number of light rail systems in the country has increased from 7 to 31 with 640 miles of track. Many new bus routes have recently opened in communities like Gwinnett County, GA; Midland/Odessa, TX; Eagle County, CO; Glendale, AZ; and Concord, NC. Major cities in 17 states are currently planning, constructing or operating bus rapid transit (BRT) services. In a survey of its members by the U.S. Conference of Mayors, 48 of the 50 major metropolitan areas are either planning or expanding rail services.

The resurgence in public transportation is primarily attributed to steady increases in investment at the federal, state and local levels. This investment has dramatically expanded and enhanced existing public transportation services, attracting more riders on state-of-the-art systems in metropolitan, suburban and rural areas.

Past generations would not recognize America's public transportation vehicles today. Vehicles are taking a departure from tradition with sleek, modern, attractive and fuel-efficient designs that still maximize passenger capacity and provide easier, low-floor boarding. Alternative fuels are making public transit even better for the environment. One example is the Regional Transportation Commission of Southern Nevada, which operates a bus modeled after a train with a diesel-electric hybrid engine that is expected to have a 22-year life as opposed to the average 12-year life of a regular bus.

Right: TRAX light rail system in Utah has exceeded ridership projections ever since it opened in 1999.

Left: A modern diesel-electric hybrid vehicle in Las Vegas.

Below: Historic street cars in San Francisco are used by both local residents and tourists.

Bottom: Commuters in Los Angeles.

Customers on transit systems of all sizes are enjoying the luxury of technological advances—including automatic vehicle locaters (AVL) and global positioning systems (GPS). These technologies enable transit systems to provide audio and visual announcements informing customers when the next bus or train will arrive, where the vehicle will stop, or if there are delays or service changes. Many transit systems are also integrating the latest technologies with their web sites and email lists giving customers up-to-the-minute information on vehicle locations and significant delays from their desks, cell phones or PDAs.

In Williamsport, PA, City Bus opened a new Trade and Transit Center with mobile data terminals (MDT) installed on the city's 28 buses. Customers can wait inside the warm, dry terminal until signs and voice announcements let them know that their bus has arrived. The Los Angeles County Metropolitan Transportation Authority (MTA) has seen a 40 percent increase in ridership on its Metro Rapid lines since it began providing riders with real-time arrival information. And, in Washington, DC, the Washington Metropolitan Area Transit Authority (WMATA) launched an eAlert customer service option enabling riders to receive an email within two minutes of a significant delay. Within the first three months of operation, 13,000 customers had subscribed to the service.

It's back to the future in communities that are bringing back the streetcars. The New Orleans Regional Transit Authority (RTA) recently opened its restored Canal Street Line with 23 new streetcars modeled after the original cars built by Perley Thomas in 1924. Even though the appearance may fool onlookers, the new cars are futuristic structurally, electronically and mechanically. The Southeastern Pennsylvania Transportation Authority (SEPTA) in Philadelphia also is

rebuilding 18 streetcars. And, of course, a trip to San Francisco is not complete without a ride on the historic cable cars which are also an essential means of travel for local residents.

The Benefits

Every segment of American society—individuals, families, communities, businesses and industries—benefits from public transportation. It enhances personal opportunities by getting people where they need to go, whether it's work, school or play. Public transportation helps all community members stay active and provides access to events and activities, creating strong personal bonds and community identity. It fosters communities where people can drive less and walk more, meeting the needs of all citizens.

transportation is far greater than the costs. This is true in urban, suburban and rural areas at the state and regional levels. The overall economic benefits of public transportation may exceed costs by as much as six to one.

Public transportation gets people to work; investment in it also creates jobs. In fact, for every $1 billion invested in public transportation infrastructure, 47,500 jobs are created or sustained. These are good-paying jobs in a variety of industries—including manufacturing, construction, finance, insurance, real estate, and retail and wholesale trade—in the regions served by public transportation and throughout the country.

In places such as Plattsburgh and Hornell, NY, and Sacramento, CA, hundreds of workers are assembling orders for rail equipment. Bus manufacturers at several locations put hundreds of people to work everyday building buses that serve rural and mid-size communities across America.

In addition to the jobs directly created by new construction or renovation of systems, are the jobs created by the ripple effect of capital investment in public transportation. New Orleans expects the economic activity generated by its Canal Line to create over 1,661 new jobs. The South Florida Regional Transportation Authority expects its five-year transit development to generate 6,300 ongoing system-related jobs in operations, maintenance and other industries.

In the last decade, there has been an increase in the trend of businesses relocating from urban to suburban and rural areas. As a result, there is a steady increase in the "reverse commute." Transit systems are connecting people to jobs and services in areas where they may not live—via improved connec-

Public transportation is an essential part of a balanced transportation system that includes walkways, bicycle paths, air service and roads. Each day, the option to ride public transportation allows Americans to make transportation choices that improve their quality of life by shortening commute time, avoiding stressful driving situations, and increasing the amount of time they can spend with family and friends.

Public transportation provides Americans the freedom to live their lives by pursuing opportunities and enjoying greater access and mobility. Ensuring this requires safety and security, which is why our nation's transit systems make the safety and security of passengers their top priority.

The overall economic stability of our country is reliant on public transportation. The return on dollars invested in public

Above: Students in Lansing, Michigan.

Right: Bus purchases throughout the country create manufacturing jobs in Wichita, Kansas and elsewhere.

"If our transit system were to suddenly stop, our metropolitan transportation operation would grind to a halt. This would make it impossible for employees to get to work and for businesses to receive and ship goods. The metropolitan economy would eventually grind to a halt as well."

—**A. Lee Blitch,** President and CEO, San Francisco Chamber of Commerce

tions between different modes of transportation. Routes are being extended to outlying suburban communities, and businesses are hiring bus shuttles to carry employees from rail lines to employer destinations.

Examples abound. For instance, in Atlanta, travelers and airline workers rely on the Metropolitan Atlanta Rapid Transit Authority (MARTA) for a 16-minute commute from downtown to the airport. In Waco, TX, a new downtown bus terminal links local, intercity, senior and rural bus service. CityBus in Lafayette, IN, built an intermodal transportation center in conjunction with Purdue University featuring easy access for public transportation users and pedestrians. This new downtown hub enables students, residents and visitors to conveniently combine walking, biking and public transportation to get to area retail stores, restaurants, movie theaters, residential dwellings, a park and a childcare center.

Increased Real Estate Value

Public transportation service is a major impetus for economic development and rising property values around stations. It keeps the heart of downtown business districts beating, from finance and commerce to retail and culture. It even helps to revitalize neglected neighborhoods.

In Washington, DC, the new $104 million New York Avenue station on Metro's existing Red Line has been built through an equal partnership among the federal and DC governments and local business interests. The station will trigger significant new mixed-use development, redeveloping an underserved part of the city.

New businesses and developers are drawn to transit stations where solid customer bases and consumer demands create an environment ripe for success. The Dallas Area Rapid Transit (DART) light rail line has generated $1.3 billion in private development in its first six years. The 35-mile MetroLink light rail system in St. Louis has sparked construction of a convention center hotel, a performing arts center and the Jackie Joyner Kersee Sports Complex.

Smaller scale bus-oriented public transportation investments are also spurring economic redevelopment. In Dayton, OH, the

Wright Stop Plaza occupies a historic building and provides easy access to, and transfers between, most routes of the Greater Dayton Regional Transit Authority. The HARTline bus system in Tampa, FL, coordinated development of its new University Area Transit Center in a chronically depressed neighborhood with development of a nearby community center and renovation of a major mall. The result is over $75 million in development near the transit center, bringing new life, and increased land values and tax revenues to the area.

The growing numbers of Americans who want to reside in "livable communities" are finding that public transportation is helping meet their needs. These communities feature safe, convenient, attractive and affordable neighborhoods. They are built around mixed uses—including work, services, and social destinations, designed to provide residents with transportation choices and reduce traffic congestion. Ultimately, livable communities enable everyone to contribute and find personal fulfillment as citizens, employees, volunteers or students.

These communities are providing enormous benefits to property owners and residential tenants because they are near public transportation. In the Chicago area, homes within a half-mile of a suburban rail station, on average, sell for $36,000 more than houses located farther away. In San Francisco, property in the metro area is averaging a premium of 20-25 percent over comparable non-transit properties. Fannie Mae, the nation's largest source of home mortgage financing, is currently piloting a program that recognizes the

Above: Dallas Area Rapid Transit's light rail system has generated over $1 billion in private development.

Right: When public transportation serves a mix of residential and commercial uses, as it does at this Caltrain stop in northern California, it helps reduce vehicle trips, makes residents less dependent on their cars and sparks new business and cultural activities.

cost savings residents reap when living near public transportation, enabling families to afford better housing options.

Relieving Traffic

While the public transportation industry reaches record growth, traffic congestion continues to choke America's roadways and restrain community and business development. Across the country, people, businesses, the economy and the environment are paying a high price for mounting congestion.

Traffic congestion is becoming a growing concern for Americans as the consequences of lost time and wasted fuel worsen. Each person traveling in peak periods wastes, on average, 46 hours a year—over five working days—in congestion delays. In 2002, congestion cost the nation $63.2 billion and individuals $1,160 in wasted fuel and time.

Increased public transportation relieves traffic congestion. Without public transportation, nationwide travel delays in 2002 would have increased by 32 percent, costing residents in the major urban areas studied an additional $20 billion in lost time and fuel. A full rail car removes 200 cars from the road, and a full bus removes 60 cars from the road. In fact, if all Americans who take public transportation to work drove alone, they would fill a nine-lane freeway from Boston to Los Angeles.

Investment priorities must dramatically shift toward the expansion of high-capacity public transportation systems to alleviate traffic congestion. In addition, transportation projects and services must be better coordinated from the design to implementation phase to ensure our highways and public transportation systems are working in concert.

The nation is also reaping savings in its energy bills as a result of public transportation. For every passenger mile traveled, public transportation is twice as fuel efficient as the private automobile. And, if Americans used public transportation at the same rate as Europeans—for roughly 10 percent of their daily needs—the U.S. would reduce dependence on foreign oil by more than 40 percent, or nearly the amount imported from Saudi Arabia each year.

Public transportation is also playing a role in creating a healthier nation. Over 140 million Americans—25 percent of whom are children—live, work and play in areas where air quality does not meet national standards. On average, public transportation produces 95 percent less carbon monoxide than the private automobile.

During the 1996 Olympic games in Atlanta, expanded public transportation services reduced morning peak auto use by 22.5 percent and drastically reduced the number of asthma-related medical visits.

With nearly 65 percent of adults in the U.S. overweight and 30 percent obese, public transportation is helping pave the way for a more active nation. In sprawling communities, where few travel options are available, cars are currently used for 80 percent of trips less than one mile in length. Transit-oriented developments and walkable communities reduce reliance on motor vehicles and promote higher levels of physical activity.

The cost of transportation to and from medical treatments is staggering, particularly in rural and small urban communities. Medicaid and Medicare pay nearly $3.5 billion a year to provide transportation to non-emergency medical treatments. It is estimated that more than half of Medicare ambulance trips, accounting for as many as 90 percent in rural areas, are for non-emergencies and can exceed $500 per trip.

Increased reliance on public transportation for travel to and from medical treatments can save millions if services are enhanced and expanded.

Communities are beginning to develop innovative solutions. The Oklahoma Healthcare Authority pays the Metropolitan Tulsa Transit Authority (MTTA) an average of only $2.19 per client per month to operate all non-emergency Medicaid

Above: Riders in our nation's capital rely on the Washington Metropolitan Area Transit Authority.

"With population growth and congestion threatening the capacity of our roadways, Chicago's central area vision plan now assumes that 70% of all new work trips into the downtown business district will be conducted via the public transportation system."

—Jerry Roper,
President and CEO, Chicagoland Chamber of Commerce

The aging population in the United States is growing faster than any other population, and 70-year old Americans today are expected to outlive their driving years by six to eight years. For many older Americans, not being able to drive is like losing a passport to their everyday world. As access and mobility among the nation's aging population become increasingly important, the public transportation industry is committed to meeting the needs of older persons and keeping pace with a growing demand.

The future of the public transportation industry, including serving the needs of the rapidly growing aging population, is dependent upon a continuation of steady increases in public transportation investment at the federal, state and local levels. Even with record high levels of investment, the American Association of State Highway and Transportation Officials (AASHTO) estimates that the public transportation industry currently faces in excess of $43 billion in capital needs each year.

Above: Public transportation provides individuals and families across America with opportunities, choice and freedom to accomplish what is important to them.

Below: Seniors ride C-TRAN in Vancouver, Washington.

transportation in the state. The Rhode Island Public Transit Authority (RIPTA) bus and paratransit service provides non-emergency transportation to all Medicaid recipients with an average cost of 45 cents per trip, the lowest in the country.

The Outlook

Increasing access to public transportation is clearly the best route to a stable, healthy and strong America, and residents in urban, suburban and rural areas alike need expanded and enhanced services. In the last decade, the public transportation industry made great strides in serving more Americans, but there inevitably will be challenges ahead.

Increased awareness of the benefits of public transportation among public and elected officials is essential to a positive outlook for the industry. With governments, community groups and all transportation entities working together, integrated transportation networks will serve the needs of individuals and communities. This will ensure that the public transportation industry lives up to its potential of providing all Americans the transportation choices they need to pursue opportunities, enjoy greater access and mobility, and live an enhanced quality of daily life.

Anil Verma Associates, Inc.

444 South Flower Street
Suite 1688
Los Angeles, CA 90071
213.624.6908
213.624.1188 (Fax)
anilverma@earthlink.net
www.anilverma.com

Anil Verma Associates, Inc.

Auburn Commuter Rail Station and Transit Center
Auburn, Washington

Left: Commuter rail station.

Middle: Pedestrian bridge.

Bottom left: Tracks and platforms wih station, parking and retail areas beyond.

Bottom right: Night view of partial station skyline.

This award-winning project in Auburn, a rapidly growing city midway between Seattle and Tacoma in the Green River Valley, is an important component of the 82-mile Sounder Commuter Rail System. Anil Verma Associates served as prime consultant for the design and development of this joint-development project. This project integrated a commuter rail station with a major bus transit center, retail shops, kiss-and-ride areas, a parking structure for 600 cars and a surface plaza forming a focal point for the entire development and the downtown community. The new buildings were designed to reflect the style of Auburn's historic buildings and the city's heritage, with a goal of attracting new businesses to the central business district. Completed in August 2000, the station includes an architectural detail found on some of the city's older buildings — the corbel. The corbels on the station structures are designed with

internal lighting that illuminates the face of the structure and the plaza. The modern glass pyramid roof-forms, which float on brick piers, are reminiscent of Native American, European and Japanese architectural forms. These cultures are associated with the city's history. A pedestrian bridge rises 28 feet above the rail tracks unifying station facilities on both sides. The central station clock tower reinforces the development's cohesive architectural forms and serves as a marker for the revitalization of the neighboring commercial district. Commercial redevelopment adjacent to the station has begun, and several new freeway access ramps now directly link the station with the surrounding communities.

Top: Pedestrain bridge with elevator stair tower.

Above middle: BusTransit center and parking structure.

Above: Station passenger canopies.

Left: Station structure roof detail and brick pier supports.

Anil Verma Associates, Inc.

Tren Urbano, Rio Piedras and University of Puerto Rico Underground Stations
San Juan, Puerto Rico

Above: Rio Piedras Station platform view.

Below: Rio Piedras Station South Headhouse entrance interior and mezzanine access.

The Tren Urbano project is the first rapid rail transit system to serve Puerto Rico. It is comprised of a 10.7-mile route connecting Bayamon, Guaynabo, Rio Piedras, Hato Rey and Santurce in San Juan. Part of this system runs at grade or on an elevated guideway and the rest in twin bored tunnels, strategically serving commercial and residential areas with the highest population density and greatest traffic congestion. This design-build contract of a heavy-rail system is a Federal Transit Administration Demonstration Project. Anil Verma Associates is the architect of record and urban designer for the underground design-build Rio Piedras Contract segment, consisting of cut-and-cover and twin bored tunnels, serving two underground stations. The Rio Piedras station is a stacked drift tunnel station with cut-and-cover entrances at each end, and the University of Puerto Rico station is totally a cut-and-cover station. The stations have center platforms, mezzanines and entrances opening out into headhouses at the street levels. There are two to three levels of ancillary spaces at each end of the stations. The Rio Piedras Station is sited in a dense commercial district with historic buildings, posing major historic and structural challenges. The University of Puerto Rico Station is located in an historic district within the University's campus. The station entrances are integrated into the historic and local urban context. The firm worked closely with community leaders to gain community support throughout the design-build process and also coordinated all the aesthetic components with the State Historic Preservation office.

Right: Rio Piedras Station north Headhouse entrance and plaza.

Below left: Entrance view from platform at University of Puerto Rico station.

Below right: Rio Piedras Station interior.

Bottom left: Tunnel construction.

Bottom right: Rio Piedras Plaza above station and South Headhouse beyond.

Anil Verma Associates, Inc.

Metro Red Line Vermont/Beverly Subway Station
Los Angeles, California

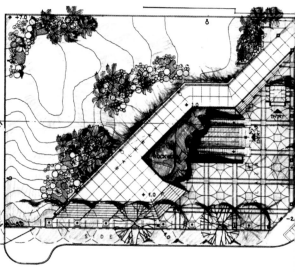

Above: Station site plan.

Above left: Station lobby with quarter round patterns.

Left: Stairway to platform with crafted rock forms as artwork.

Facing page top: Drawing of station exterior.

Facing page bottom: Drawing of station interior-platform level.

The Vermont/Beverly Station is on the 17-mile Metro Red Line subway system that provides service between Union Station and the San Fernando Valley through Downtown, the Mid Wilshire area, and Hollywood. This underground station has a 450-foot platform with ancillary facilities at both ends of the platform, at the mezzanine level, and a level above the mezzanine. Escalators, elevators and stairs lead from the street level to the underground facilities. Anil Verma Associates, Inc. served as the project's prime contractor, project manager, and architect-of-record for final architecture and engineering design. The station box employed cut-and-cover construction with twin bored tunnels, entailing major utility relocations, underpinning of adjacent buildings, and maintaining normal traffic operations during construction. The firm initiated significant cost-saving measures during the design phase, including eliminating a projected 60-foot exten-

sion of the station box by reconfiguring ancillary spaces, and then further reducing a proposed 30-foot extension to 15 feet for a planned future station entry. The station architecture applies quarter-circular forms found on prominent nearby structures as a motif throughout the plaza and station areas. Working with a local artist, the designers have incorporated crafted indigenous rock forms as sculptural elements on the plaza and within the platform area.

Anil Verma Associates, Inc.

South Sacramento Corridor Light Rail
Sacramento, California

This light rail corridor originates in downtown Sacramento and extends 6.3 miles to Meadowview Road. The 2003 opening of the South Line represents the first phase of a two-phased 11.2-mile extension of the existing light rail line south to Elk Grove. Anil Verma Associates, Inc. was a 50-percent partner on a construction management team for the project which consist of double tracks, seven stations, utility systems, grade crossings, signals, communications, traction power, overhead catenary system, electrical power, parking and park-and-ride facilities, highway overpass and relocation of the previous Union Pacific Railroad tracks out of the corridor. As it passes through upscale as well as less affluent neighborhoods, the trolley is intended to transport workers to industrial areas, students to classes at Sacramento City College and state workers to jobs downtown. Each station is designed to relate to the visual, cultural and historic context of its specific neighborhood.

Above: South Line Meadowview Station

Below: North Hollywood Tunnel Segment.

Below right: North Hollywood Station platform.

North Hollywood Metro Red Line-Segment III Tunnel and Stations
Los Angeles, California

This heavy-rail subway project consists of 6.3 miles of twin-bored tunnels complete with cut-and-cover passenger stations extending from the terminus of Segment II at the Hollywood/Vine Station to a new terminus at the North Hollywood Station. Anil Verma Associates, Inc. was a subconsultant to a Joint Venture providing construction management services between Hollywood/ Vine and Universal City stations. The firm had specific responsibilities for the construction of tunnels and stations.

Booz Allen Hamilton

8283 Greensboro Drive
McLean, VA 22102
703.902.5000
703.902.3333 (Fax)
www.boozallen.com

Booz Allen Hamilton

Booz Allen Hamilton

Metro Gold Line Light Rail Transit
Los Angeles, California

Left: Gold Line Memorial Park
Station and artwork.

Below: Lake Station and Metro
Rail train.

Right: Gold Line terminus at Sierra Madre Villa Station.

Photography: Booz Allen Hamilton.

The 13.7-mile Metro Gold Line, inaugurated in 2003, connects to multiple other transit systems at Union Station in downtown Los Angeles. The line extends from there through Chinatown, Highland Park and Mount Washington to Pasadena. The system includes 13 stations and a maintenance and storage facility, a half-mile aerial structure, two cut-and-cover tunnels, a pedestrian highway over-crossing, two parking garages, traction power and an overhead catenary system. Booz Allen and its team of subconsultants served as the Program Management Consultant for all phases of the project. After analyzing alternative procurement strategies, the team recommended a design-build approach and prepared the Request for Proposal, contract, scope of work, technical specifications and engineering drawings. From cost estimating and project controls to community outreach, integration of artworks and environmental mitigation, the Booz Allen team provided oversight for the award-winning project, which was completed on time and on budget.

Booz Allen Hamilton

The River LINE
Camden to Trenton, New Jersey

Above: Light rail vehicle delivery via cargo airplane.

Right: River LINE maintenance facility.

The 34-mile, 20-station River LINE light rail system connects Camden and Trenton along an historic and environmentally sensitive freight right-of-way. The project goal is to boost economic development in a depressed corridor and relieve traffic congestion while improving connections to other transit modes. Booz Allen has worked on every major stage of the project including developing a procurement strategy, preparing a business plan and contract documents, preparing operations and maintenance requirements, initiating safety and security planning and supporting the environmental impact analysis. The firm also provided preliminary engineering for the diesel-powered light rail vehicles, signaling, traffic control, communications and fare system. This work led to the awarding of a design-build-operate-maintain contract to a joint venture. Subsequent to the award, Booz Allen provided services in program and contract management, oversight of vehicle and systems engineering, systems integration, safety and security, and operations and maintenance. This included system safety certification, review of timetables, crew and vehicle assignments and

maintenance procedures. Several complex elements figured in the success of the project. Among these, the rail line combines freight and passenger use, placing strict safety requirements on the system. The historic and environmental features of the right-of-way required close coordination with responsible state and federal agencies. Wetlands and wildlife, including nesting bald eagles and spawning fish, needed to be preserved and protected during design, construction and installation of the system. The firm also conducted a study of a possible one-mile extension of the system to the State Capitol in the center of Trenton, and is overseeing the transition from design-build to operations. A significant feature of the project was the first use of diesel-powered light rail in the U.S. As part of the integrated approach, Booz Allen designed the system for vehicles to operate in three modes: exclusive right-of-way, on tracks shared with freight traffic and intermingled with highway traffic.

Above: Track through natural sites.

Right: Easy-access station platform.

Below: Camden Waterfront Entertainment Center Station.

Photography: Andy Ryan, Andy Ryan Photography, Inc.; Steve Bonina, Booz Allen Hamiliton.

Booz Allen Hamilton

TransLink® Regional Fare Card Program
San Francisco Bay Area

Left: One smart card system for ferries, buses and rail.

Below left: TransLink® add-value machine.

Below left middle: TransLink personal card reader.

Bottom left: TransLink platform card reader at ferry terminal.

Photography: Rick Butz, Booz Allen Hamilton.

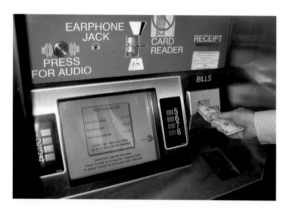

More than two dozen different transit agencies serve the 7 million residents and nearly 4 million annual tourists in the Bay Area. The Metropolitan Transportation Commission (MTC), the nine-county region's coordinating and financing agency for public transportation, has been researching, developing, testing and implementing a regional fare collection program based on a "smartcard" system that works across multiple modes of transit, including bus, train, light rail, subway and ferry. Booz Allen has assisted at every stage including developing detailed system specifications and a quality assurance plan and overseeing equipment and system integration and installation. After considering and then rejecting a magnetic-stripe ticket system, the firm investigated the smart card alternative. Working with partner agencies and with manage-

ment and technical assistance from Booz Allen, MTC moved forward with its TransLink® smart card program through an innovative design-build-operate-maintain approach to contracting and procurement. Now in the implementation phase, TransLink currently integrates six agencies with multiple transportation modes. Plans call for more than 20 agencies to participate in the program by 2010.

Booz Allen Hamilton

Metrorail and Metrobus Information Technology Renewal
Washington, DC

The Washington Metropolitan Area Transit Authority's (WMATA's) Information Technology Renewal Program is underway to upgrade and integrate the information technology aspects of Metrobus and Metrorail operations. The effort is designed to integrate databases to improve system access, flexibility and responsiveness. Other benefits include more efficient data entry, improved business processes, more reliable scheduling and dispatch of buses and trains and more reliance on preventive maintenance and advanced inventory planning systems. To maximize industry best practices and avoid unnecessary maintenance and training costs for customized software, the project team has selected and is implementing commercial off-the-shelf applications for bus and rail scheduling and dispatch; human resources and payroll; accounting, budgeting and capital procurement; and maintenance and material management. These applications form an integrated system that also integrates with legacy systems. As the systems integrator for the project, Booz Allen is providing services for the system's requirements validation, design and testing, as well as its implementation and deployment. The firm is also providing change-management services to transform the organization and realize the maximum benefits from the new systems.

Above: Metrorail and Metrobus systems business operations upgrades.

Top right: Bus and rail scheduling and dispatch improvements.

Right: Increased Metrorail operating efficiencies.

Below right: Coordination of maintenance and material management.

Photography: Larry Levine, WMATA.

Booz Allen Hamilton

London Underground Improvements
London, United Kingdom

Booz Allen serves as a prime consultant to Tube Lines, a private consortium responsible for the maintenance of and improvements to the London Underground, for the re-signaling of the Jubilee, Northern and Piccadilly lines. The project is the largest re-signaling effort in the rail transit industry's history. Part of a $7 billion, 7-year upgrade to this 43-mile portion of the Underground system, this phase encompasses systems engineering and integration, procurement and contracting assistance and technical specification development for a new transmission-based train control (TBTC) system. When complete, the Underground's upgrade will enable additional carrying capacity, decrease travel time and substantially reduce delays while improving reliability and safety. The re-signaling project requires completion of the upgrade without interrupting service—involving installing, testing and commissioning the TBTC equipment during the four-hour nightly shutdown period.

Above: Delivery of Jubilee Line rolling stock for testing.

Right: Improvements to rolling stock, track, train control, signaling and stations.

Photography: Booz Allen Hamilton.

CH2M HILL

9191 South Jamaica Street
Englewood, CO 80112
877.741.5221 (Toll Free)
720.286.9250 (Fax)
www.ch2mhill.com

CH2M HILL

CH2M HILL

Regional Transportation District
Southwest Light Rail Line
Littleton/Denver, Colorado

The 8.7 mile Southwest Light Rail Line, which opened in July 2000, extended the system from the I-25/Broadway Station—the previous end of the line for Denver's original Central Corridor Light Rail Line—to Mineral Avenue in the City of Littleton. The firm provided the Regional Transportation District with a fast-track environmental impact statement evaluating environmental and socioeconomic effects of both build and no-build alternatives for a number of different criteria. The assessment also included one of the first comprehensive evaluations of environmental justice issues associated with implementing the project. Preparing the environmental impact statement involved extensive public hearings and community meetings. Subsequently, the firm evaluated an approximately two-mile extension of the Southwest Corridor into Highlands Ranch, including consideration of alternative routes and environmental tradeoffs. The firm provided planning analysis and conceptual design for the new track, two new stations, park-and-ride facilities for 1,400 cars and an intermodal transfer facility to access a proposed commuter rail line from Castle Rock, Colorado.

Top: Light rail corridor.

Above: Littleton/Mineral Station.

Left: Southwest Line.

Photography: Steve Nayowith.

CH2M HILL

Utah Transit Authority
University and Medical Center Light Rail Transit Lines
Salt Lake City, Utah

CH2M HILL led the design joint venture on the design-build team for the award-winning extension of the Utah Transit Authority's TRAX light rail network to the University of Utah's Rice-Eccles Stadium in Salt Lake City. The team met the critical goal of having the new University Line running ahead of schedule, in time for the 2002 Winter Olympics. The transit system moved more than 4 million riders during the Games. The University Line project included design and construction of two and one-half miles of track, four stations, a half grand union, two double crossovers, roadway and intersection reconstruction and numerous utility relocations. The design team developed innovative approaches to save time and money, most significantly using an aggressive pavement milling and overlay program to minimize pavement reconstruction. The same team then extended the line 1.5 miles farther to the University's Health Sciences Center. This second project included one side- and two center-platform stations, a single and a double crossover, plus roadway and utility work.

Top: University Line.

Above: Medical Center extension.

Left: Rice-Eccles Stadium station.

Photography: Fred Wright; SLC Rail Constructors (aerials).

CH2M HILL

Sound Transit
Central Link Light Rail
Seattle, Washington

With its three stations, the 4.3-mile-long, double-track rail segment of the Central Link Light Rail transit system through the Rainier Valley in South Seattle will be an integral part of the system's initial line. The line will connect downtown Seattle, the industrial area south of downtown, and residential and commercial neighborhoods in Beacon Hill, the Rainier Valley, Tukwila, and SeaTac. By 2020, Link trains are projected to carry at least 42,500 riders a day. This segment will run from South Walden Street at street level in the center median of Martin Luther King Jr. Way South to Boeing Access Road. It will traverse a predominantly residential area with multiple commercial districts. The project requires widening the corridor enough to include the trackway, a four-lane arterial roadway with left turn pockets, and sidewalks. Managing and minimizing the numerous property impacts associated with the project will be critical to its success. Special urban design elements include development of plazas, integration of public artworks and creation of new pedes-

Left and below: Existing and proposed corridor sections with corridor improvements and retaining wall design. (Retaining wall artwork by Dick Elliott.)

trian and bicycle facilities. The firm provided civil engineering final design and construction support services for road and track alignments, three stations, several new pedestrian crossings, three sizable retaining walls, inter-section plans, drainage, and public and private utility relocation.

Left and below: Changes at location of proposed Edmunds/Columbia City Station.

Renderings: CH2M HILL (this page); Company 39 (facing page).

CH2M HILL

City of Albuquerque Transit Department
West Side Transit Facility
Albuquerque, New Mexico

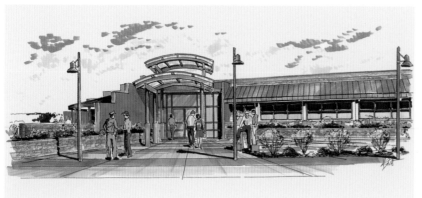

Above: Main entrance and operations center.

Below: Maintenance building and garage.

Renderings: DWL Architects & Planners, Inc. of New Mexico.

The new Transit Facility will provide the fast-growing population on Albuquerque's West Side with a new bus maintenance and operations center to reduce the deadhead time and mileage to and from route service. An operating garage for 140 buses and 35 paratransit vans, the new facility will also provide future capability for an alternative-fueled, compressed natural gas fleet and the City's articulated buses for the system's Bus Rapid Transit service. The firm's role covers facility programming, site planning, final design and construction services. Among major components in the new facility: canopy parking for the revenue fleet, vehicle maintenance shops, operator and supervisor facilities, and complete vehicle servicing facilities. The multiphase project will also provide central component repair and paint and body facilities for the entire transit system.

CH2M HILL

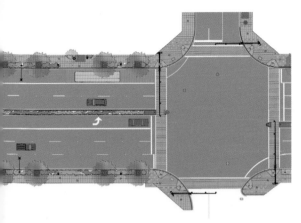

Above: Aurora Avenue and N. 165th Street Intersection.

Right: Corridor before.

Below right: After project improvements.

Photography/visualizations: CH2M HILL; CAD intersection by Arai Jackson Ellison Murakami LLP (above).

This new roadway design for a three-mile stretch of SR 99 (Aurora Avenue North) will provide much-needed improvements for pedestrians and traffic while taking into consideration the goals and values of all stakeholders along the corridor. The current avenue is marked by traffic congestion, aging strip development, poor access to transit services and a lack of pedestrian facilities. Previous attempts by others to improve and redevelop the corridor failed to reach consensus in support of a plan. To develop a new roadway supported by all elements of the community, the firm pioneered the use of context-sensitive solutions practices to aid in designing an environmentally sound roadway that would be acceptable to the salmon community of the Northwest as well as those utilizing the roadway corridor.

Representatives from the firm, local agencies and businesses, along with more than 600 citizens, participated in 34 project meetings that resulted in a widely supported plan that adds business-access and transit lanes in both directions with transit signal priority, a landscaped median with focused left-turn lanes and a 12-foot, continuous sidewalk zone with safer bus stops and shelters, and improved connections to trails and local commerce. The transit improvements are initial-stage elements for an 11-mile Bus Rapid Transit line to be implemented on Aurora Avenue.

CH2M HILL

Orange County Transportation Authority
I-5 High Occupancy Vehicle (HOV) Lane Widening
Orange County, California

The firm provided design services for the I-5 High Occupancy Vehicle (HOV) lane widening project from Pacific Coast Highway (SR 1) to El Toro Road. The project added one HOV lane in each direction and modified the existing roadway, structures and interchanges to accommodate the new lanes. Changes to the highway included on-ramp HOV bypass lanes and California Highway Patrol enforcement areas. The northern two miles allow for two HOV lanes and an auxiliary lane in each direction between interchanges. Traffic management during construction on this major highway required extensive planning. Design elements included 26 structures, changeable message signs, widening and metering on-ramps for 11 interchanges, soundwalls up to 16 feet high, retaining walls and the highway patrol enforcement areas. The changes to the highway necessitated modifications to 100 drainage systems requiring extensive planning and permitting.

Above: Double HOV lanes.
Below: HOV lane entry.
Photography: Robert Holmes.

DaimlerChrysler Commercial Buses North America

6012 High Point Road
Greensboro, NC 27407
800.882.8054
www.dcbusna.com

DaimlerChrysler Commercial Buses North America

DaimlerChrysler Commercial Buses North America

Orion VII

Atlanta, New York, Sacramento, Toronto, Washington, DC and elsewhere

Left: Orion VII bus in service in Toronto.

Right, below: Orion VII low floor, advanced-technology bus.

DaimlerChrysler Commercial Buses North America offers a wide-range of buses and coaches – from the Sprinter Shuttle to the S 417 motor-coach. As part of the world's largest commercial vehicle manufacturer, DCCBNA delivers vehicles with innovative engineering, design and technology to keep its customers ahead of the competition. Its newest innovation, the heavy-duty Orion VII low-floor bus, has been designed from the ground up to optimize passenger safety and comfort. In addition, it provides the operator with unparalleled reliability, efficiency, and ease of maintenance. Available in 30-, 35- and 40-foot models, the Orion VII leads the industry in passenger comfort and carrying capacity. Its multi-plexed electrical system simplifies diagnostics and maintenance too. The Orion VII is offered with a stainless steel frame and has proven itself at the grueling Altoona federal bus testing facility as well as through an extremely challenging 500,000 mile "shaker" test program. In addition to building durable and reliable vehicles, Orion has been a leader in alternative fueled transit buses. In the late 1990s, Orion introduced its hybrid-electric buses to the industry. Buses fueled with clean diesel, CNG, and the exciting hybrid electric propulsion system from BAE Systems give customers the power of choice, while offering impressive benefits to passengers, operators, and to the environment. More than 1,000 Orion VII buses have been ordered since introduction in 2001. Washington Metro Area Transit Authority (WMATA) has ordered 250 Orion VII CNG-fueled buses for 2005 delivery. Nearly 600 of WMATA's current 1,500-bus fleet were manufactured by Orion. When the new Orion

VII buses go into service, WMATA will have the distinction of being the only transit authority in the United States that has every Orion model in operation. Toronto Transit Commission took delivery of 220 Orion VII clean diesel buses in 2004 and has ordered 250 more starting delivery in 2005. Hybrid electric buses that have been delivered to customers for evaluation, have successfully accumulated more than half a million miles in revenue-service operation. MTA New York City Transit ordered 325 Orion VII hybrid electric buses and already has many of them in operation.

Right: Fully accessible entry.

Below: Hybrid electric propulsion Orion VII in New York City.

Photography: Michael Coughlan (below).

DaimlerChrysler Commercial Buses
North America

Setra S 417

Left: European designed, German engineered Setra S 417.

Right: Elegant design inside and out.

Below: Reclining seats and tray table options.

Center: Indirect ceiling lighting.

Bottom: S 417 in Atlanta.

Setra of North America, markets and distributes new and pre-owned European-designed and German-engineered luxury coaches throughout North America. The S 417 features a sophisticated interior and exterior design, seating for up to 58 passengers and an ergonomic and efficient driver cockpit. The ceiling's indirect lighting enhances the height of the cabin. The coach offers leading-edge technological systems, including a fully integrated multiplex electronic system with comprehensive on-board diagnostics. Setra first introduced the TopClass S 417 HDH in 2001 and it was awarded the honor of Coach of the Year the following year at BusWorld in Kortrijk, Belgium. In February of 2003, Setra introduced the North American designed S 417 luxury motorcoach. Customized for the North American market, this coach is 45 feet long with a width of 102 inches. The coach is built with a low-emission Detroit Diesel Series 60 engine and an Allison B500R transmission. Currently, there are around 2,600 TopClass S 417 HDH coaches gracing European highways and an estimated 220 S 417 motorcoaches in operation in North America. This represents a market share of 30% in the North American luxury motorcoach market. The following are a few of the companies in America that have adopted the S 417 motorcoach: A Yankee Line, Arrow Stage Lines, and Premier Coach Company.

DaimlerChrysler Commercial Buses
North America

SLF 200
San Bernardino; Lexington; Cleveland;
Prince George's County, Maryland

The SLF 200 mid-sized bus is designed for the diverse demands of low-floor bus applications. Recognized for its high level of performance, reliability and durability, it is offered in 29-, 32- and 35-foot lengths, in a variety of floor plans, and clean diesel, CNG and propane fuel options. A kneeling feature with a step-in height of only 9 inches, 40-inch-wide doors and broad aisles make boarding faster and safer for passengers. In combination with the durable, lightweight all-aluminum body, an exclusive Mercedes-Benz engine delivers an exceptional power-to-weight advantage and better fuel efficiency. The Class 1 multiplexed electrical network and on-board diagnostics reduces downtime and operational costs. Its maneuverability and tight turning radius have made the SLF 200 popular in both city and suburban environments, including Omnitrans, Transit Authority of Lexington (LexTrans), Greater Cleveland Regional Transit Authority, and Prince George's County (Maryland) Transit. It is Altoona tested for 12 years, 500,000 miles.

Right: Spacious interior with an extra-wide aisle.

Far right: Kneeling feature with paratransit ramp.

Below right: Maneuverability in urban congestion.

Below: SLF 200 35-foot length.

Facing page top: Low-floor design and wide doors.

DaimlerChrysler Commercial Buses North America

Sprinter Shuttle
Toledo, Ohio; Randleman, North Carolina; Nashville; Jacksonville, Florida

Left: Select floor plan with spacious luggage areas.

Below: Sprinter Shuttle.

The Sprinter Shuttle seats up to 12 passengers and features an advanced Mercedes-Benz MBE 600 diesel engine and 5-speed automatic transmission. The fuel-efficient powertrain operates with extended maintenance intervals and up to 22 miles per gallon on most routes. Sprinter option packages, which are designed for specific application needs, include parking, hotel, valet and paratransit styles. All models feature 36-inch, full-view entry doors that open outward for better passenger clearance. Along with full-height interiors, the Sprinter Shuttle offers passengers a spacious cabin, comfortable seating and superior ride quality. Independent suspension, shock-absorber struts and axles provide improved traction, stability and road adhesion. It is available in both single and dual rear-wheel models. The driver's cockpit is ergonomically designed with easy to reach controls and adjustable seat. A wide variety of organizations have selected the Sprinter, including the University of Toledo, Holiday Tours, Grayline-Nashville, and Runways Shuttle.

David Evans and Associates, Inc.

2100 SW River Parkway
Portland, OR 97201
503.223.6663
503.223.2701 (Fax)
www.deainc.com

David Evans and Associates, Inc.

Airport MAX Light Rail Extension
Portland, Oregon

Left: Airport MAX Red Line on I-205 bridge.

Below left: Light rail train near Portland International Airport.

Below center: Mount Hood behind Airport MAX train.

Facing page top right: Parkrose park-and-ride light rail train station.

Facing page bottom right: Parkrose Station and pedestrian bridge.

Photography: Bob Pool Photography.

This 5.5-mile extension of TriMet's Metropolitan Area Express (MAX) Red Line from the existing Gateway Transit Center along the I-205 corridor to the Portland International Airport includes four new stations, accommodations for a future platform and modifications to the Gateway Park-and-Ride Station. The project also added a seven-span, 1,200-foot "flyover" bridge from the I-205 median over the southbound travel lanes and a 500-foot bridge carrying light rail, pedestrians and bicycle traffic over I-84. DEA served as the prime engineer and lead designer on the design-build team, participating in the conceptual, preliminary and final design and construction phases, providing civil, bridge, traffic, environmental and structural engineering. The integrated design-build approach and use of innovative building techniques enabled the team to begin construction before completion of design. Airport MAX combines public and private financing, a first for a major U.S. transit line. The innovative partnership provides for future transit-oriented development on 120 acres near the airport. Winner of the Project of the Year Award from the American Public Works Association and other honors, the complex project required fitting tracks within the existing median and through the airport complex. The line is projected to carry 2.7 million riders annually by 2015.

David Evans and Associates, Inc. Interstate MAX Light Rail Extension LS10C Segment
Portland, Oregon

Left: Interstate MAX 4,000-foot-long Vanport Bridge.

Below: Light rail vehicles at Expo Center Station.

Facing page top: Vanport Bridge over environmentally-sensitive Columbia Slough.

Facing page center: One of several artist-created timber gates, or torii, at site of Japanese-American internment camp.

Facing page bottom: Sculpture at Delta Park Station.

Photography: Bob Pool Photography.

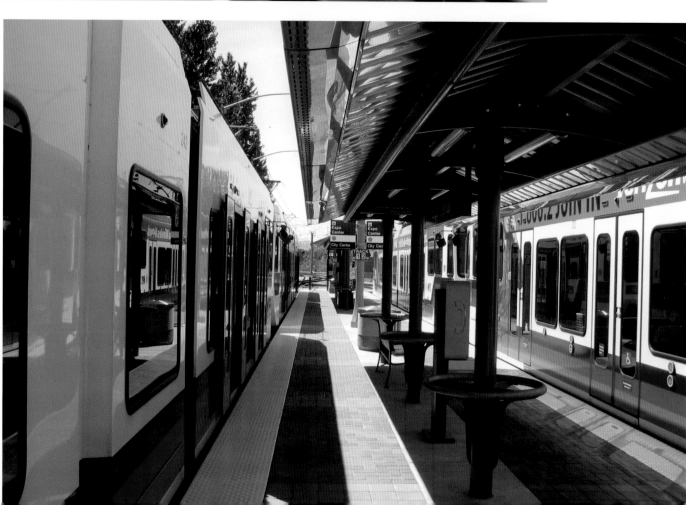

Part of the 5.8-mile extension of Portland's 44-mile light rail system, this 8,200-foot, northernmost section of the Interstate MAX Yellow Line includes 4,000 elevated feet of dual track and two new stations with park-and-ride facilities. As prime engineer for the design-build team, the firm was responsible for design management, engineering design, survey work, permitting and construction engineering. The 28-span Vanport Bridge includes piers in the environmentally sensitive Columbia Slough that required fast-track approaches to meet restricted in-water work periods for construction. To enhance the structure's ability to serve under lateral train and seismic forces, the team developed a unique structural system using the continuous welded rail as a structural member to tie the separate bridge units together. The innovative system significantly reduced the cost of the bridge's substructure. The at-grade section required reconstruction of existing roadways and relocation of sanitary sewer and water lines while maintaining traffic to busy adjacent facilities. The team worked closely with artists commissioned to create artwork for the project, including artwork that recalls the history of the Japanese-American internment during World War II and a flood that devastated the region six decades ago. Interstate MAX is the winner of the 2005 Project of the Year award from the American Council of Engineering Companies of Oregon (ACEC Oregon).

45

David Evans and Associates, Inc.

America's national parks are environmentally sensitive areas visited by millions of people each year. The sites require protection while visitors interact with their natural, cultural and other attractions. As park usage has increased, visitors often struggle to find parking spaces and face traffic jams, which can mar the park experience and harm its special environment. The firm is leading a multidiscipline team providing visitor management strategies and transportation planning, design and implementation services to the National Park Service for parks throughout the U.S. and its territories. Among the many projects are evaluation of water-borne transportation systems for the Channel Islands National Park, development of plans for improvements to Grand Canyon rim shuttle buses and evaluation of bus and light rail alternatives, multimodal access and circulation planning for Yosemite Valley and analysis of transportation system alternatives for Hawaii Volcanoes. The planning and project development process has been tailored to the specific needs of each park. Solutions are intended to blend into the park environment, enhancing rather than detracting from the visitor's experience. The firm's team recommended changes to parking management, public transit, roadways and trail systems. In addition, operating schedules and new routes for transit systems are being established to reduce waiting times. Each project utilizes site-appropriate sustainable design elements and materials.

Facing page top: Grand Canyon National Park shuttle fleet.

Facing page bottom left and right: Grand Canyon informational displays at Canyon View Plaza.

Top: Yosemite National Park shuttle bus.

Above: Yosemite National Park Valley Shuttle.

Below: Grand Canyon shuttle bus.

Photography: National Park Service and David Evans and Associates, Inc.

David Evans and Associates, Inc.   Spokane Regional Light Rail Project
Spokane, Washington

The firm serves as the prime consultant on a General Management and Engineering Consultant team assembled to perform alternatives analysis leading to the selection of the preferred alternative for development of a high-capacity transit system serving the 16-mile South Valley Corridor. The team also created concepts for transit-oriented developments along the corridor. This line, extending from downtown Spokane to the City of Liberty Lake, would be the starter line in a proposed regional light rail system. Alternatives developed include a range of light rail transit applications as well as bus rapid transit options, streetcars and combinations of different modes. A full corridor light rail system would have 15 stations and 23 electric vehicles; a minimum operable segment of light rail would extend 7.8 miles and include eight stations and five diesel vehicles; and a complete bus rapid transit system would have 12 station pairs and 14 vehicles. The project includes evaluation of a variety of alignment conditions and presentation of visual simulations and animations for the public education process.

Above: Simulation of light rail intersection crossing.

Right: Bus rapid transit alternative at intersection.

Far right: Electric streetcar alternative with shared right-of-way.

Below: Transit-oriented development concept for new city center.

Simulations: 3D animation stills, Newlands and Company, www.nc3d.com

DMJM Harris, Inc.

An AECOM Company

605 Third Avenue
New York, NY 10158
212.973.2900
212.697.2329 (Fax)

515 South Flower Street
Ninth Floor
Los Angeles, CA 90017
213.593.8200
213.593.8601 (Fax)

www.dmjmharris.com

Above: Crossing improvements.

Top right: Fort Lauderdale
International Airport Station.

Below right: Increased corridor
speed.

Photography: John Livzey.

A 72-mile railroad line, the South Florida Rail Corridor runs through the Miami, Fort Lauderdale and West Palm Beach region. Trains from the TRI-RAIL commuter, Amtrak intercity and CSXT freight lines operate on the heavily trafficked corridor. The firm serves as project manager for three separate design-build corridor improvement projects. For the first, Segment 5, the firm prepared the design-build procurement documents, administered the competitive bid process and provided construction management for 44 miles of double-track construction, 24 bridges, 10 stations and 70 at-grade full closure crossings. The improvements will reduce peak period headway times to 20 minutes, enhance grade crossing safety and improve on-time operational performance. Significant modifications to the horizontal geometry of the existing and new mainline tracks provide for raising the maximum authorized speed for passenger trains to 90 miles per hour. The New River Bridge project phase includes the design and construction of a high-level double-track bridge over the south fork of the New River in Broward County. This bridge for TRI-RAIL and Amtrak trains will supplement the existing bascule bridge, which will continue to be used by CSXT. The third project will construct 3.6 miles of 22-foot-high precast concrete sound barrier walls in seven segments. The barriers will mitigate traffic noise from the adjacent Interstate 95 roadway and shield neighboring residences from train traffic sound.

DMJM Harris, Inc.

Second Avenue Subway
New York, New York

Left: 57th Street Station rendering.

Center: 57th Street Station interior rendering.

Bottom: Second Avenue Subway line construction segments.

Renderings: DMJM Harris*Arup.

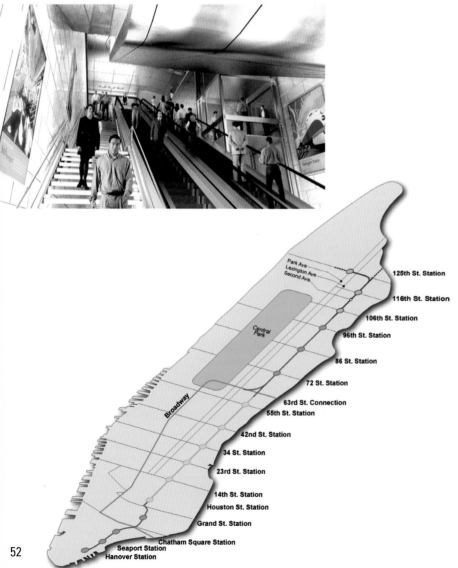

The new Second Avenue Subway is designed to ease the massive congestion Manhattan's East Side subway riders presently face. The new subway line will follow Second Avenue 8.5 miles, north to south, from a terminal station at 125th Street to Whitehall Street in the Financial District. The two-bore tunnels and 16 stations will connect to the existing subway system at seven locations, the MetroNorth Railroad at 125th Street, and the existing bus system at almost every stop. When the first segment opens in 2011, initial ridership is projected to be 202,000 daily. The entire $16.8 billion line is expected to serve 560,000 riders daily when complete. As a joint venture partner, the firm is responsible for the preliminary engineering of the entire alignment. The team also provided engineering input for the environmental impact statement process. Various tunneling methods will be used, including tunnel boring, cut-and-cover and mining techniques. As part of a four phase project, the team initially developed as part of the first phase, a design-build contract for a bored tunnel between 96th Street and Midtown. The next steps will include final design of all stations for the first phase and construction engineering services.

DMJM Harris, Inc.

Frank R. Lautenberg Rail Station at Secaucus Junction
Secaucus, New Jersey

This complex and massive rail infrastructure project constructed the Frank R. Lautenberg Rail Station at Secaucus Junction, a major rail transfer station, and expanded the Northeast Corridor from two to four tracks for approximately 10,000 feet between the Portal and Bergen interlockings. The new station is located at the juncture of the busiest stretch of railroad in the country at the Northeast Corridor and New Jersey Transit's Main Line and Bergen County Lines and now allows for easy transfer to trains bound for Manhattan's Penn Station. As the centerpiece of a planned transportation and commercial development, the complex will eventually include office, hotel and retail space and associated roads and parking. The firm won several awards for the comprehensive construction management services it provided for the three-level, 312,000 square-foot station, 20 miles of new track with an elevated viaduct structure including 20 new bridges and four interlockings and construction of all signal and transmission power systems.

Above left: Lautenberg Rail Station interior.

Above: Station exterior.

Left: Station platforms.

Photography: John Livzey (above left); Vanessa Petrizzi (above and left).

DMJM Harris, Inc.

Washington Metro
Washington, DC

The Metro, which currently serves 700,000 daily riders on its 103 route miles, needs to grow to meet the demand for extended mass transit service in the Capitol District region. The firm is providing general engineering and architectural services for several major capital and repair and rehabilitation projects. Among them are the Core Capacity Study, a capital plan that will serve as the roadmap for expansion and refinement of the system for the next 25 years. The firm also prepared design documents and procurement strategies for the 3.1-mile, design-build Largo extension of the Blue Line in Maryland, including two stations, a 2,200-car parking structure and significant urban design elements to mitigate impact on the surrounding community.
A 24-mile extension of the system will construct an entirely new line along the

Dulles International Airport Corridor from West Falls Church through the airport and into Loudoun County. For the Dulles line, the firm is providing preliminary engineering, environmental services, program management, civil, structural and systems design, operating plans and cost estimates. On the Red Line in downtown Washington, the New York Avenue Station will be the system's first in-fill station and first update in station design in 30 years. The firm provided design services including staging plans to ensure smooth cutover into the existing system.

Left: Metro College Park Station.

Above: Metro tunnel station.

Below: Elevated train line.

Bottom: Metro tunnel station.

Photography: DMJM Harris.

DMJM Harris, Inc.

Metrolink Commuter Rail System
Southern California

Left and below left: Metrolink five-county system.

Below: Passenger and freight line.

Photography: DMJM Harris.

Since Metrolink's inception in 1990, the firm has continuously provided Southern California's five-county commuter rail system with planning, preliminary engineering, final design, engineering, program management and construction management services. The largest commuter rail start-up in the United States in more than 50 years, the Metrolink system now comprises more than 600 track-miles serving more than 38,000 passengers on seven different lines daily. With freight and passenger service operating on shared rights-of-way, the firm developed designs for new and rehabilitated track to carry commuter rail traffic at 79 miles per hour. The firm has designed and managed construction of more than 200 miles of new track, upgrade of 40 freight sidings, 25 new bridges, including the one-mile San Gabriel River flyover, multiple bridge and right-of-way drainage improvements, as well as upgraded channels and structures crossing the right-of-way. The firm also developed new signal and communications systems, improvements to more than 70 grade crossings, and other major right-of-way improvements.

Edwards and Kelcey

299 Madison Avenue
PO Box. 1936
Morristown, NJ 07962
973.267.0555
973.267.3555 (Fax)
www.ekcorp.com

Edwards and Kelcey

Frank R. Lautenberg Rail Station at Secaucus Junction
Secaucus, New Jersey

Below: Column-free concourse.
Bottom: Aerial view of station.

Located west of New York City near the popular Meadowlands Sports Complex, the Rail Station is one of New Jersey's premiere transportation hubs and the interconnecting point for 10 of 11 New Jersey Transit commuter rail lines serving northern New Jersey. The three-level station is located at the juncture of Amtrak's Northeast Corridor—the busiest stretch of railroad in the Northeast—and New Jersey Transit's Main Line and Bergen County Line. The station's soaring column-free, skylighted concourse provides access to train platforms, curbside drop-offs and a planned office/hotel development above the station site. The project required expansion of the Northeast Corridor from two to four tracks for approximately two miles, with the outside tracks reserved for high-speed (100 mph) through-service and the interior tracks for local trains. Environmental restrictions and soil conditions required the use of viaduct to support a large portion of the rail expansion. Deep foundations were needed to support the railroad and station. Major work also included high-speed turnouts to enable Amtrak trains stopping at the station to enter and leave the mainline fast enough to avoid disruption of intercity rail service. The firm's responsibilities for the project included conceptual planning, environmental assessment, operations analysis and preliminary and final design work.

Left: Vehicle drop-off access.

Below: New commuter and Amtrak platforms.

Photography: Michael Rosenthal/New Jersey Transit.

Edwards and Kelcey

Highbridge Yard and Shop
Bronx, New York

Above: Yard along Harlem River.

Right: Aerial view.

Above: Maintenance facility.

Right: Yard entrance.

Photography: Edwards and Kelcey; Harry Armand/ Washington Group.

Metro-North Railroad (MNR) and Long Island Rail Road (LIRR) are designing a new link to New York City's Grand Central Terminal to improve access to Manhattan's East Side and reduce congestion for commuters in the busy Long Island transportation corridor. The multi-year, multi-billion-dollar program will eventually route trains through seven miles of new tunnels into a new LIRR commuter station to be built beneath Grand Central

Terminal, owned and operated by MNR. A major component of this program, construction of the Highbridge Yard and Shop transformed a derelict rail freight yard along the Harlem River into a modern electrified rail yard for midday storage of electrical multiple unit and diesel-hauled trains for Metro-North Railroad. A design-build project, the new yard provides train storage, servicing and maintenance facilities, replacing Metro-North's

facilities formerly within Grand Central Terminal. The new yard provides MNR, the nation's second busiest commuter railroad, with seven miles of storage and service track and 20 switches, storage space for 100 rail cars, a two-track, 900-foot-long maintenance building with an 8,300-square-foot office building, an attached 900-foot-long train shed, a 16-megawatt substation, a state-of-the-art diesel fueling facility, and an

employee rail station with an overpass bridge over the three mainline tracks. The riverside site's high water table necessitated raising the entire, mile-long site three feet above the 100-year flood plain. As lead engineer, the firm managed the overall design effort, rail operations coordination and project staging.

Edwards and Kelcey

Hiawatha Corridor Light Rail Transit System
Minneapolis, Minnesota

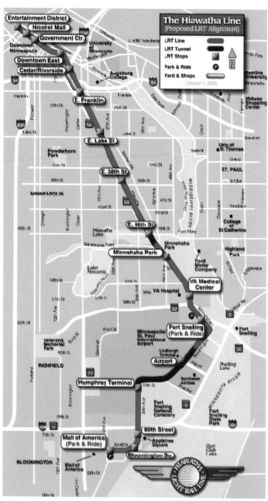

The opening of the Hiawatha Corridor Line introduces an attractive, fast, congestion-easing transportation alternative into a busy Twin Cities corridor. The $715 million system provides rapid access from downtown Minneapolis to the Mall of America, a major tourist destination in Bloomington, via the Minneapolis/St. Paul International Airport. The 11.6-mile line features 17 passenger stations— 12 in Minneapolis, three in Bloomington and two at the airport. The transit system is designed not as a classic "commuter line" that runs through a downtown to large clusters of suburban homes at either end, but as a "development line" that will encourage growth in the corridor and extension of rail and bus connections to St. Paul and suburban areas. The Hiawatha Line will initially serve an estimated 19,300 passengers, increasing to 25,000 by 2020. The $320 million Minnesota Transit Constructors design-build project included design and construction of civil works, trackwork, traction power, signal and communication systems, traffic control and management systems, an operations and maintenance facility and 15 passenger stations. Edwards and Kelcey's role included civil engineering, track and utility relocation, structural design of bridges and walls, signals and communications, traction power and overall system quality.

Above: Government station.

Top Left: Hiawatha Corridor line.

Left: Light rail tracks.

Center left: Metro Transit LRT.

Far left: Operations facility and link to downtown.

Photography: Edwards and Kelcey; Hiawatha Project Office.

Edwards and Kelcey

Lake Street Interlocking Project
Chicago Union Station
Chicago, Illinois

One of the nation's most revered train stations, Chicago's Union Station opened in 1881 and remains an essential link for Amtrak's intercity passenger service and the region's heavily traveled commuter rail system. The north side of the station is controlled by the Lake Street Interlocking where, each day, more than 350 trains and deadheads move through three mainline tracks to ten station- and two through-tracks to the station's south side. The Lake Street Interlocking has over three miles of new track, 52 electric switches with snow-melters, new signal power, vital microprocessor signal technology, reconstructed subgrade and drainage systems, and clearance improvements throughout the overbuild portions. A new consolidated control center, located in Amtrak's 14th Street Yard, controls the Interlocking remotely. The firm planned and designed all track work for the project.

Edwards and Kelcey

23-Mile Rail Extension Project
Worcester, Massachusetts

Left: Commuter station.
Above: Pedestrian bridge.
Center left: New mainline tracks.
Below left: Station construction.
Photography: Edwards and Kelcey.

With the goal of connecting Massachusetts' two largest cities—Boston and Worcester—the Massachusetts Bay Transportation Authority (MBTA) extended commuter rail service from Framingham to Worcester along an existing 23-mile rail corridor. The MBTA now serves an additional 2,500 commuters per day. The new line shares traffic with Conrail freight and Amtrak intercity rail service. Development of the corridor required construction of four commuter rail stations with parking, roadway and pedestrian access; upgrade of the existing tracks including four new interlockings; addition of 11 miles of a second mainline track; improvements to

signal and communications systems; inspections, rating and improvements to 20 bridges including replacement of one and major rehabilitation of others; construction of a layover facility, complete with power distribution system, and a terminus in Worcester; and traffic improvements at grade crossings. Design of interim commuter facilities and track work enabled the much-needed rail service to begin as quickly as possible while final construction continued. The firm served as project manager and coordinator for the design team and had responsibility for all civil engineering and structural design work.

Fox & Fowle Architects

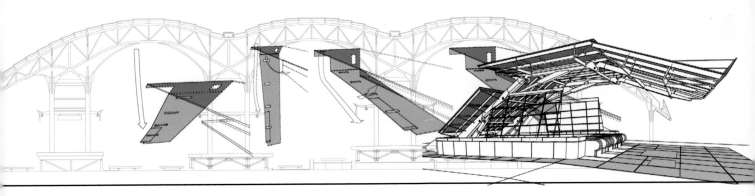

22 West 19th Street
New York
New York 10011
212.627.1700
212.463.8716 (Fax)
www.foxfowle.com

Fox & Fowle Architects

Fox & Fowle Architects

Times Square Subway Station
New York, New York

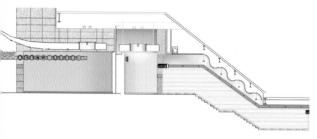

Main Entrance

The main entrance of the Times Square subway station captures the area's exuberance with a vibrant, undulating canopy, topped with brightly-lit animated signs. The forms announce the subway's presence on the street and orient passersby to the 11 subway lines that the station serves. The canopy leads passengers down into the station, evoking an appropriate sense of motion. On the track level, a curved lighting and sign element, suggesting an old Broadway theater marquee, brings the flavor of Times Square street life into the heart of the station. This marquee is the focal point of the station and helps to orient the subway rider within the station complex.

Reuters Building Entrance

The Reuters Building features a covered entrance and connecting stair to the Times Square subway system. A projecting canopy announces the entry with an animated, illuminated S-U-B-W-A-Y sign. Designed for maximum visibility within this busy neighborhood, the nine transit lines that converge beneath Times Square are identified at street level by an armature combining wayfinding with the neon vernacular of the area. The design developed for this subway entrance addresses the Transit Authority's standards for the station, which is under complete renovation.

Above: Times Square station signage and section.

Right: Reuters Building entrance.

Photography: Roger Whitehouse, (above); Fox & Fowle Architects, (right).

Fox & Fowle Architects

Roosevelt Avenue Intermodal Station
Queens, New York

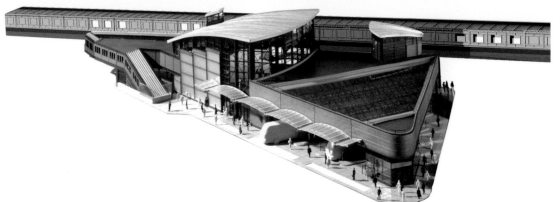

Above: Terminal renderings.

Left: Model photography by Lydia Gould Bessler.

Below left: Arcing roof at night, under construction.

Below center: Skylights.

Below right: Louvered windows.

Renderings: Fox & Fowle Architects.

The Roosevelt Avenue Intermodal Terminal serves as an entrance and transfer point between elevated and subgrade New York subway lines and buses to LaGuardia Airport and other destinations in the metropolitan area. The design of the terminal building, rooted in the historic infrastructure, provides a modern beacon for the diverse urban neighborhood. The roof arcs up into the shape of a large fan, bringing graceful lines to the utilitarian, industrial materials. Various glazing techniques, blue-green terra cotta panels, robust steel detailing, and engaging geometry create a compelling space form and identifiable civic space. The space functions as a natural chimney; natural ventilation draws warm air up through the station and vents it out through louvered windows. A skylight system allows daylight penetration while incorporating integrated photovoltaics to power below grade lighting systems. Photovoltaics are incorporated into roofs of the headhouse and the elevated platform, as indicated in the green guidelines for the entire system authored by the firm. The two neighborhoods on either side of the station provided valuable input into the design process, making the new terminal a valuable centerpiece at the heart of the community. The project is under construction.

Fox & Fowle Architects

Second Avenue Subway Line
New York, New York

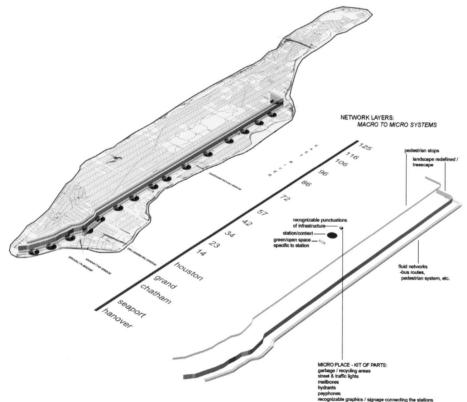

NETWORK LAYERS:
MACRO TO MICRO SYSTEMS

125
116
106
96
86
72
57
42
34
23
14

houston
grand
chatham
seaport
hanover

pedestrian stops
landscape redefined /
treescape

recognizable punctuations
of infrastructure
station/context
green/open space
specific to station

fluid networks
-bus routes,
  pedestrian system, etc.

MICRO PLACE - KIT OF PARTS:
garbage / recycling areas
street & traffic lights
mailboxes
hydrants
payphones
recognizable graphics / signage connecting the stations

Top left and right: Entrances
at 86th Street.

Above: System diagram.

Right: 86th Street station
rendering.

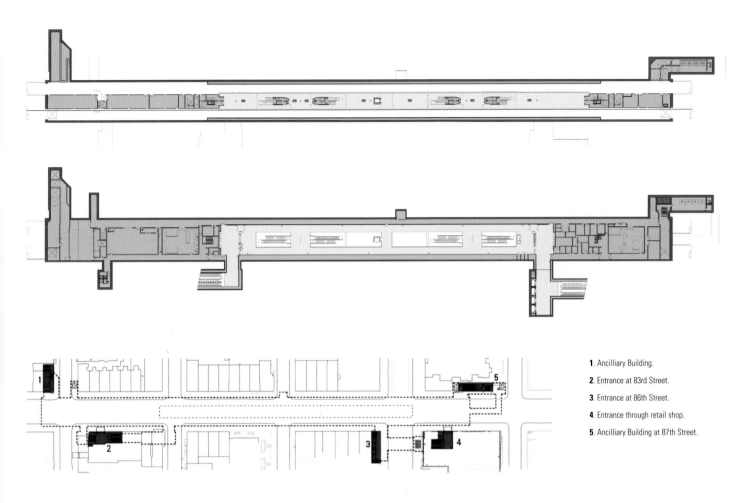

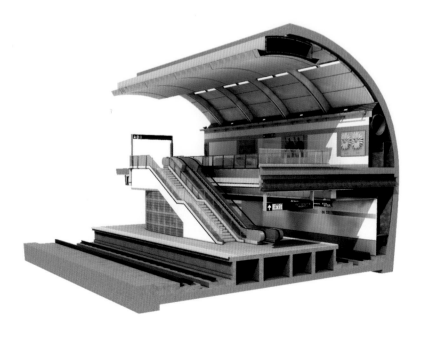

1. Ancilliary Building.

2. Entrance at 83rd Street.

3. Entrance at 86th Street.

4. Entrance through retail shop.

5. Ancilliary Building at 87th Street.

Above: 86th Street station plan and map

Below: Station cutaway rendering.

The new Second Avenue Subway line will run from 125th Street to Whitehall Street, the full length of Manhattan's East Side. The firm is designing the stations with New York City Transit's goals in mind: environmental responsibility, high-performance design, neighborhood integration, and maintainability, in the context of creating a system that meets passengers' needs for security, ease, and comfort. Above ground, the new stations will engage the identity of the line as a whole, as well as embrace each neighborhood's unique character. The final resolutions for the stations will contain significant elements of commonality through universal plat-form, canopy, and enclosure components. For variability and to create a sense of identity for each of the diverse neighborhoods, each station design will integrate community-responsive art installations. The new line will capture the energy and enthusiasm of the city and provide an exciting experience for tourists and residents alike.

Fox & Fowle Architects

Hoboken Light Rail Station
Hoboken, New Jersey

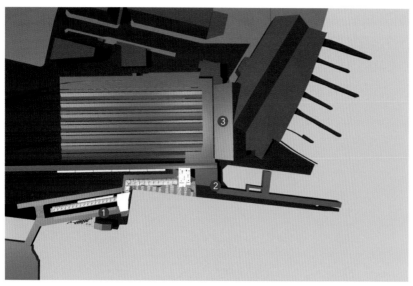

1. Lightrail Station.

2. Ferry Terminal.

3. Rail Terminal.

Above left: Hoboken waterfront site plan.

Above right: Station platform.

Right: Column and cable-suspension structure.

Below right: Glass block windscreens on platform.

Photography: Richard Caden.

The Hoboken Station, one of several the firm has designed for the Hudson-Bergen Light Rail Transit System, is a new terminal sited on a central waterfront site in the heart of historic Hoboken. It provides a link for residents of New Jersey's Hudson and Bergen counties to commuter trains, PATH trains, and ferries, as well as pedestrian access to members of both the adjacent communities of Hoboken and Newport. The location of the station on the waterfront recaptures the waterfront for public use, creating public open space and providing a convenient intermodal connection. The project team inserted a modern transit structure into the historic context, creating dynamism and balance. The open structure borrows from the traditional train station vocabulary and makes reference to nautical shapes and forms. Curved glass block windscreens along each platform allow for wind protection for both seating and ticket machines. The column and cable-suspension structure is contemporary, providing a conscious aesthetic contrast to the nearby buildings of historic Hoboken. The design also incorporates works of art into the composition; the combination of elements forms an exciting new object within the Hoboken waterfront landscape.

Fox & Fowle Architects

Bergenline Avenue Tunnel Station
Union City, New Jersey

Below: Site plan.
Bottom: Station rendering.
Renderings: Fox & Fowle Architects.

The Bergenline Avenue Tunnel Station will serve as an important intermodal station stop on the Hudson-Bergen Light Rail System. This is the system's only tunnel station, constructed within an existing train tunnel through the Palisades with platforms 160 feet below ground and an expansive plaza at the street. The open plaza will provide a contrast to the dense urban context of Union City and West New York and form an important open space in the community. Access to the platform below is provided by elevators within the brick and glass headhouse structure, and vent stacks and a sleek glass canopy span the length of the plaza. The vent stacks have integrated lighting that will emit a subtle glow during the evening hours. The basic palette of the station of brick, stone, glass, and metal relates to the adjacent community's existing buildings materials and scale. At the track level, the 300-foot-long platforms will have a high arcing ceiling with some rock of the tunnel partially exposed. A number of artists, including Alison Sky, were employed to incorporate art throughout the platform level; the effort includes two- and three-dimensional works. The project is under construction.

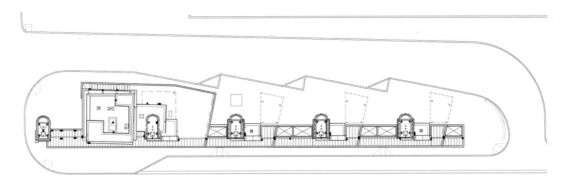

Fox & Fowle Architects

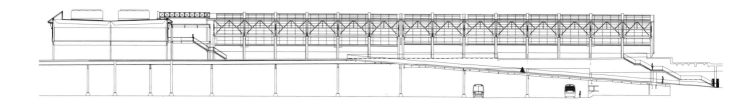

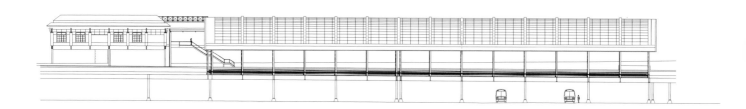

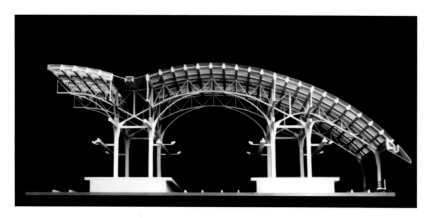

Stillwell Avenue Terminal
Brooklyn, New York

The Stillwell Avenue Terminal required a complete structural overhaul and improvements to circulation; accessibility, security, and architectural expression were investigated. Four new glass elevators were proposed to serve all platform levels, to demarcate the sta-tion's location from a distance. A large roof canopy unifies the platforms and tracks, articulated with integrated photovoltaic panels for supplemental electrical power needs. This conceptual study positioned the Stillwell Avenue Terminal as a catalyst for future redevelopment in the area.

Top: Stillwell Avenue Terminal sections.

Above: Model of canopy roof.

Right: Light Rail line map and platform rendering.

Renderings: Fox & Fowle Architects.

Newark-Elizabeth Light Rail Stations
Newark, New Jersey

The first operating segment of this new light rail line, now under construction, links Newark's Penn Station, Performing Arts Center, new multi-purpose sports stadium, and Broad Street commuter rail station, with an advanced, forward-looking network.

Gruen Associates

6330 San Vicente Boulevard
Suite 200
Los Angeles, CA 90048
323.937.4270
323.937.6001 (Fax)
carbrey@gruenassociates.com
www.gruenassociates.com

Gruen Associates

Gruen Associates

Los Angeles to Pasadena Metro Gold Line
Los Angeles County, California

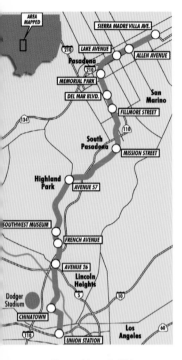

Above: Metro Gold Line system map.

Below: Memorial Park Station and rendering.

Above: Southwest Museum Station.
Below: Highland Park Station.

The first new light rail project in Los Angeles County in more than a decade, the Gold Line links 13 neighborhoods and connects Pasadena to Downtown Los Angeles. Its 14-mile, 13-station route captures Southern California's rich history of diversity from historic Olvera Street and Chinatown to the small-town appeal of South Pasadena's Mission Street to the cultural centers of Pasadena. Constructed within a former Santa Fe Railroad right of way, the project included a maintenance yard, restoration of an historic bridge over the Arroyo Seco, two cut-and-cover underpasses—one through historic Old Pasadena—two surface park-and-ride lots, and an Intermodal Transit Center with a 1,000-car parking structure. Gruen Associates prepared the bid documentation for the station and landscape design to be implemented through a design-build contract. Site-specific art by a wide variety of local artists lends the stations individual identities. Gruen reviewed design-build drawings for design intent, ensuring the implementation of the publicly accepted design. Since its opening day in June 2003, the Line has attracted a large ridership.

Above right: Southwest Museum Station.

Right and below: Mission Street Station and rendering.

Bottom: Cypress Park Station and rendering.

Photography: Gruen Associates.

Renderings: George Bungarda.

Gruen Associates

Santa Monica Boulevard Transit Parkway
West Los Angeles, California

Left: Existing conditions.

Right: Typical intersection.

Below: Projected completed boulevard.

Photography: Gruen Associates.

Rendering: John Messer.

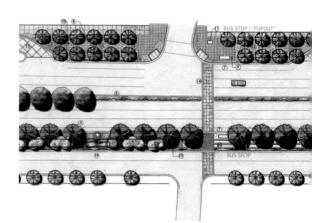

A multidisciplinary team prepared alternatives to improve traffic flow, provide space for bus transit and bicycles and enhance the aesthetic character and identity of "big" and "little" Santa Monica Boulevard, a major West Los Angeles thoroughfare long lacking in urbane character. Working closely with the neighboring communities, the firm provided urban and landscape design and environmental impact services. The project will transform a neglected area of two parallel streets and an abandoned right-of-way into a classic grand boulevard. The resulting multi-modal thoroughfare will have three lanes and a bike lane on both sides of a landscaped center median with tree-lined neighborhood-access roadways and parking along either side of the main roadway.

Gruen Associates

CenterLine Urban Rail Corridor Projects
Fullerton and Costa Mesa, California

Orange County aims to stimulate development in its underutilized urban corridors being connected by the planned CenterLine Light Rail Line. Various master plan and station design concepts were developed using New Urbanist design principles. The City of Fullerton project included a transit-oriented, mixed-use development combining a light rail station, high-density housing, neighborhood retail and offices around an existing transportation center. The proposed elevated rail station will be linked by a bridge with the transportation center and a network of open spaces. The City of Costa Mesa South Coast Plaza Station project calls for development of multiuse Transit Village on an 80-acre site to include an entertainment center, office and retail space focused on pedestrian streets. Also planned are 2,000 housing units, a series of open spaces and a five-acre park.

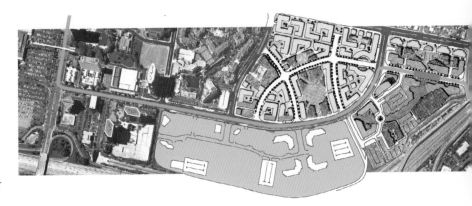

Top: Transit Village.

Above: South Coast Plaza Station concept.

Right: South Coast Plaza Station alternative concept.

Rendering and Photography: Gruen Associates.

Gruen Associates   San Fernando Valley East-West Bus Rapid Transitway
Los Angeles, California

Top: Typical view.

Above and left: Tampa Avenue before and after.

Below and bottom left: Chandler Boulevard before and after.

Bottom right: 13 mile route.

Photography: Gruen Associates.

Rendering: George Bungarda.

This award-winning project will create 13 miles of "busway within a greenway." The project will transform an abandoned, barren former railroad right-of-way into exclusive busway lanes and a bikeway/pedestrian path within a linear greenbelt to provide attractive rapid transit service across the fast-growing San Fernando Valley. The busway lanes will remove buses from normal street traffic and reduce their delays due to street congestion. Further speeding bus traffic, corridor buses will have priority at intersections. The 13 stations along its length will link important regional centers that include North Hollywood, Metro Rail Station, Warner Center, and other major destinations. The design for the transitway addressed concerns of the individual neighborhoods along its route. Each station is designed to resemble rail stations, with new pedestrian crossings and amenities, canopied seating, large trees and public art. Park-and-ride lots will provide a total of 3,000 spaces at six stations. Feeder bus lines will provide access to the transitway for Valley residents. Not only will the new corridor improve public transit, the project will create a linear greenbelt park in the Valley. Over 4,000 new trees will be planted along with drought-tolerant groundcover, providing needed shade and relief from the Valley's often intense sun. Twelve-foot high sound walls with landscaped earthen berms to reduce their visual impact will screen the busway and protect adjoining neighborhoods. Gruen Associates headed the consultant team preparing the MIS, developing conceptual/urban design engineering plans and station concepts, and assessing the environmental impacts of the BRT project.

Gruen Associates

Bus Rapid Transit Station Plan
Orange County, California

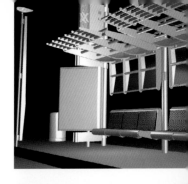

Above and right: Typical transit center with multiple shelters.

Far right: Station shelter views.

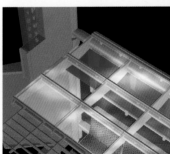

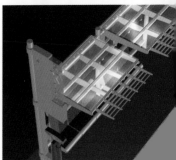

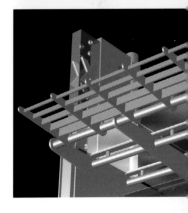

As the firm in charge of programming, urban, architectural and landscape design, Gruen Associates developed a station design plan for 60 miles along two bus rapid transit (BRT) demonstration corridors. The program proposes 40 stations, including 18 standard stations, six major destinations, three new transit centers, an existing transit center and 11 stops with station markers only. The La Brea to Newport Beach and the Long Beach to Santa Ana Lines will traverse ten cities, linking diverse settlements such as densely urban downtown Santa Ana, suburban Garden Grove and the exclusive beach community of Newport Beach. Thus this award-winning program needed to appeal to a wide-range of patrons and geographical conditions. Features of the BRT lines include limited stop operation, changeable message signs, new station canopies, a distinctive bus and specific marketing and branding. Major program components include a durable, easily maintained 12-piece "kit-of-parts" station that will shelter patrons from weather and adjust to sun angles and sidewalk widths, along with pedestrian amenities to enhance the transit environment.

Gruen Associates

Grossmont Trolley Station Transit-Oriented Development Plan
La Mesa, California

Above: Public plaza.

Left: Residential condominiums with retail below.

Below: Site plan.

Rendering: Barry Zauss.

The firm's development master plan and design guidelines for this seven-acre site directly adjacent to the Grossmont Trolley Line Station of the San Diego Trolley Line encourage transit-oriented development with four development scenarios. The plans call for the existing station and a future Mission Valley Extension to be integrated into a mixed-use development of up to five stories, with new retail and restaurants, residential complexes and parking for approximately 1,200 vehicles. The plan accommodates an existing 600-space parking agreement on the site for a local movie theater and trolley patrons. The development will rise adjacent to single-family neighborhoods across Fletcher Parkway from the site. Disabled access was also created to the nearby Grossmont Center, a major shopping mall on an adjacent bluff.

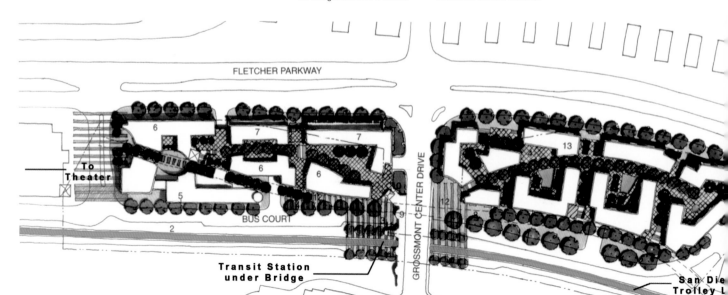

The HNTB Companies

Headquarters:
715 Kirk Drive
Kansas City, MO 64105
816.472.1201
816.472.5004 (Fax)

More than 60 offices nationwide

www.hntb.com

The Bay Area Rapid Transit (BART) San Francisco International Airport extension extended the subway line from Colma to Millbrae and linked the entire system to the region's most important airport and the fast-growing South Bay area. The largest BART project ever awarded and the largest of five nationwide Federal Transportation Administration-sponsored design-build demonstration projects, it also included new stations at San Bruno and South San Francisco. HNTB served as primary designer and was responsible for delivery of buildable plans. Eight miles of underground subway were built, along with more than a mile of aerial bridge structures serving the airport. The design-build team assumed new and unconventional roles, including primary responsibility for scheduling, coordinating, quality assurance and regulatory compliance. The team also performed final track design and systems integration services. The new line crosses beneath 20 city streets. The extension has eliminated an estimated 10,000 daily automobile trips to the airport, providing a significant boost to the region's efforts to relieve traffic congestion and comply with air-quality regulations.

Top right: San Bruno Station entrance.

Top left: San Bruno Station interiors.

Above: San Bruno Station platform.

Right: San Bruno Station lobby.

Photography: HNTB.

The HNTB Companies

South Station Transportation Center
Boston, Massachusetts

Within walking distance of downtown Boston's financial and retail center, the Transportation Center unified national bus carriers, major regional bus carriers, and commuter bus operations serving 12,000 passengers daily in a single site. Part of the historic South Station complex, it also connects bus passengers to subway and commuter rail, Amtrak and taxis. A new skylighted bus terminal and parking were built on air-rights above the railroad tracks and platforms. Work consisted of two structural decks, bus terminal operations facilities and parking, and a set of roadway ramps from the local street network with direct connections to the highway interchange of the new Central Artery and the Massachusetts Turnpike. Other elements include a new railroad and bus operations service facility, two additional railroad tracks and platforms, and extension of the South Station Headhouse, which includes a bus terminal lobby entrance. The new Center links to the Headhouse via a 255-foot canopied walkway and a 100-foot extension to the bus terminal. HNTB provided architectural, engineering and construction services for the entire project.

Top right: South Station entry.

Above: New tracks and platforms.

Below: Roadway ramp.

Right: Intermodal Transportation Center, South Station at far end.

Photography: HNTB.

The HNTB Companies

Big Four Depot/Riehle Plaza
Lafayette, Indiana

After relocation of the tracks prevented marketable reuse of Lafayette's 1902 historic railroad station, the building was moved four blocks at the architects' recommendation to a new site along the relocated tracks close to downtown and overlooking the Wabash River. The Depot now serves as the centerpiece of an intermodal transportation facility and as an indoor and outdoor public events space. With foot-and-a-half-thick limestone and brick walls, the 112 foot-long, 547-ton building was one of the largest structures ever moved. In its new location, the restored building provides 6,000-square feet of meeting and special event space above a distinctly new structure containing train and intercity and local bus transportation facilities. An elliptical plaza and grand staircase create a community gathering space connected by walkways to the Main Street Bridge, which was converted into a pedestrian public space linking the city to neighboring West Lafayette. New elevator towers providing access to the train platforms and the bridge serve as visible landmarks for the development. HNTB provided architectural and landscape architecture and design services from design development through construction administration.

Top left: Plaza entry to interior public space.

Center left: Elevator tower and stairs.

Left: Train platform and terrace.

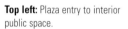

Left: Public event in Riehle Plaza.

Below: Station and pedestrian bridge.

Photography: Dave Preston, Gary Quesada.

The HNTB Companies

Charlotte 2025 Land Use/Transit Plan
Charlotte, North Carolina

One of the nation's fastest growing metropolitan areas, Charlotte-Mecklenburg faces major highway congestion threatening to choke off its strong economic growth as a national banking and financial center. The 2025 plan lays out five mass transit corridors to develop a workable growth strategy for the region. Drawing on extensive public participation and frequent interactions with local officials and the Transit Planning Advisory Committee, the plan developed by HNTB recommends bus rapid transit in three of the five corridors and rail in the other two. With growth focused in the transit corridors, the plan calls for specific techniques and incentives to align projected growth with transit station development. Central to the 2025 strategy, interim five-

and ten-year plans coordinate the phasing-in of the transit service and land development initiatives. Public outreach under the firm's guidance during the planning process included newsletters, website postings, small group presentations and broadcast interviews, yielding widespread discussion and regional support for the process. Many of the recommendations found in the final plan grew directly out of local input. As a result, the plan served as the cornerstone of a successful half-cent sales tax referendum to support its implementation.

Above: Five mass transit corridors.

Right: Proposed rail corridor.

Drawings: HNTB.

The HNTB Companies

Minneapolis-St. Paul Light Rail Transit Tunnels and Station
Minneapolis, Minnesota

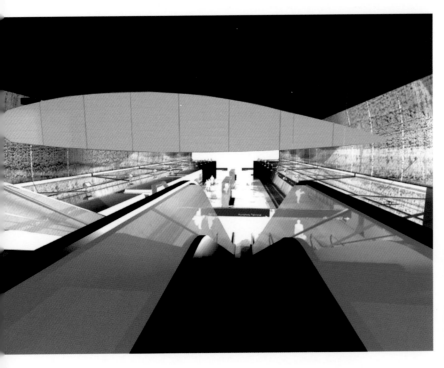

Top right: Light rail station construction.

Right: Tunnel boring.

Left and below right: Airport terminal station.

Bottom: Route of rail transit tunnel.

Photography: HGA.

Part of a multi-year regional transit improvement program, the light rail transit tunnels and station will link the Minneapolis-St. Paul International Airport to the new Hiawatha Light Rail system running from downtown Minneapolis to the Mall of America. Sixty-six feet below grade, the station at the airport's Lindbergh Terminal will be 500 feet long and lined with precast concrete walls and ceiling panels. At its center, the two-story platform provides a series of elevators, escalators and stairs to move passengers swiftly to their destinations in the terminal.

HNTB's responsibilities for the tunnel and station include tunnel design engineering, construction services and project management. Geological conditions required use of three innovative mining methods for the tunnels. When complete, the 11.6-mile Hiawatha LRT route will include 17 stations and is expected to carry more than 19,000 passengers daily. By 2020, the line is anticipated to generate more than 67,000 new jobs.

The HNTB Companies

Leonard P. Zakim Bunker Hill Bridge
Boston, Massachusetts

Below: Night view of bridge shortly before opening.

Photography: HNTB.

The Charles River crossing's slender, inverted Y-shaped towers soar 270 feet above the roadway. Along with the span's unique cable geometry, they have created a new visual icon on the Boston skyline. A dramatic nighttime lighting scheme and a planned series of parks and recreation areas at its base further solidify the bridge's place in the city's fabric. HNTB served as final design consultant and engineer of record, and provided construction management services. Designed to ease traffic gridlock on the heavily traveled Boston thoroughfares, the bridge features eight mainline lanes and two roadway lanes cantilevered outside the eastern plane of cables. At 183 feet, the structure is the widest cable-stayed bridge in the world and the first in North America to feature both an asymmetrical design and a hybrid composition of steel in the 745-foot main span and concrete in the bridge back spans. Site constraints included an active subway line and historic water main and a very limited foundation footprint.

Hubner Manufacturing Corporation

355 Wando Place Drive
Mt. Pleasant, SC 29464
843.849.9400
843.849.9404 (Fax)
info@hubner-usa.com
www.hubner-usa.com

Hubner Manufacturing Corporation   Articulation Systems and Folding Bellows for Buses
Worldwide

Hubner's articulation systems provide a flexible connection between extended buses. This connection offers many benefits to customers. Besides doubling the carrying and revenue capacity of a typical bus, it also allows buses to navigate narrow urban streets previously unreachable. Leading international bus manufacturers, such as New Flyer Industries, Neoplan, and NABI, have implemented Hubner's articulation solutions for their project needs. Why? Because the Hubner solution provides customers with a clear interface between the articulation system and the chassis. Furthermore, customized applications can be adapted to different types of chassis. Articulation systems are available for both low- and high-floor buses. Low-floor systems accommodate heights below 400 millimeters. Two versions of bottom covering are available – pocket corners or duplex ply. Both versions offer greater extension and flexibility. Hubner possesses exceptional expertise in dampening systems for articulation joints. Available systems range from mechanical shock absorbers to digital controllers. Hubner's redundant dampening system also includes an emergency-brak-

ing feature. Hubner's folding bellows are made in the USA and can be manufactured in a variety of fabrics to meet different regulatory requirements for smoke emission, flammability and toxicity. Systems are delivered ready to install, including articulation, passenger plate form, folding bellow, energy dampening system and interior parts.

Facing page top: Articulated bus.

Facing page bottom: Folding bellows in bus interior.

Top: Bellows exterior.

Right and right center: Articulation of bus exterior

Below: Articulation system diagram.

Bottom left: Articulation of bus interior.

Bottom middle: Tight cornering.

Bottom right: Articulation joint.

Photography: U. and I. Schmelzer.

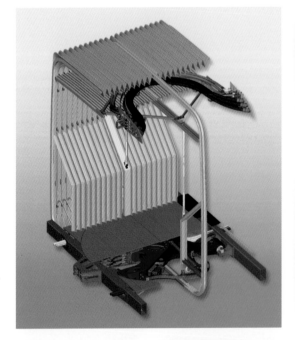

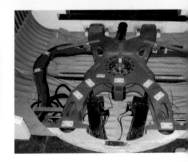

Hubner Manufacturing Corporation
Articulation Systems and Folding Bellows for Monorails
Las Vegas, Nevada; Seattle, Washington

Right: Seattle Monorail.

Below and bottom right: Las Vegas Monorail.

Photography:
Seattle, U.Schmelzer;
Las Vegas, sponsored by
Bombardier Transportation.

Seattle's elevated monorail represented the future of mass transit when it opened in 1962. The monorail runs approximately 0.9 miles and still provides a crucial link between downtown Seattle and the Seattle Center, site of the 1962 World's Fair and now home to many cultural, entertainment, and recre-

ational facilities. The monorail's two original trains are still in service. As a result of Hubner's industry experience and engineering expertise, it was called upon to replace the monorail's worn and obsolete bellows because of their unique requirements. Hubner worked closely with the City of Seattle to pro-

duce customized bellows from 45-year old drawings. Due to the exceptionally large dimensions – 15 feet high by 15 feet wide – specialized equipment and parts were required. The Las Vegas monorail glides above traffic between the Sahara and MGM resorts at 50 miles per hour in only 14

minutes. Unlike the attached covering used for the Seattle monorail, the Las Vegas monorail employs a flexible bellow cover. Further extensions are under planning.

Hubner Manufacturing Corporation

Canopy and Bellows for Jet Gangways
Worldwide

Hubner's flexible covers serve as protective passageways connecting jet gangways from terminal to aircraft. From the rounded contours of small airplanes to the nearly straight contours of jumbo jets, Hubner's two-point kinematic system ensures a safe and close seal between the folding bellow bumper and the contour of almost any aircraft. The two-point kinematics guarantees that the turning point of the upper telescopic spring is placed so that no contact takes place between mechanical parts and the airplane surface. The bellows provide a comfortable, stable and safe transitional space from the terminal into the aircraft. Bellows are available in a range of fireproof fabrics that meet all regulatory requirements. Hubner's bumpers are filled with soft polyester foam to protect the surface area of the plane.

Hubner Manufacturing Corporation

Passage Way Systems for Trains and Light Rail Vehicles
Houston, Texas; Sacramento, California; Minneapolis, Minnesota; and elsewhere

Left: Houston's METRO light rail.

Below Left: Minnesota's Hiawatha light rail.

Facing page top: Gangway inside light rail vehicle.

Facing page middle: Light rail articulation including bellow.

Below and facing page bottom: Sacramento's light rail.

Photography: U. Schmelzer.

Hubner's gangways provide a flexible connection that is designed to absorb movements between individual cars of the train or light rail vehicle. For decades, Hubner gangway systems have been implemented in railway operations and transit systems worldwide. The company offers a complete solution for car connections to ensure safe, comfortable and durable passageways that are nearly maintenance free. A passageway system may consist of a folding bellow or a corrugated bellow.

Additional features available include connecting frames, articulation systems, bridge plates and chain bridges. All Hubner products meet the requirements of vehicle manufacturers and operators for flammability and sound insulation as well as for abrasion, tensile and bending forces. For underground and urban light rail systems, Hubner passageways offer exceptional sound insulation, flame- and vandalism-resistance, and large passageway widths for comfort and maintenance. Hubner's passage-

way systems are compliant with Buy America provisions. They have been installed in major transit systems such as the Houston Light Rail and Amtrak's high speed Acela.

Left: Acela high speed train bellows interior.

Below: Acela high speed train bellows exterior.

Photography: U. Schmelzer.

Interfleet Technology

Interfleet Technology Inc.
125 Strafford Avenue
Suite 130
Wayne, PA 19087
610.225.0120
610.225.0121 (Fax)
frawley.t@interfleetinc.com

Interfleet Technology Ltd.
Interfleet House
Pride Parkway
Derby
DE24 8HX United Kingdom
44 (0) 1332.223.345
44 (0) 1332.223.331 (Fax)
www.interfleet-technology.com

Interfleet Technology

Heathrow Express
Project Management and Engineering
London, United Kingdom

Left photos: Heathrow Express.

Below: Paddington Station terminus.

Right: Siemens Class 332 electric multiple unit.

Photography: Rail Images.

Every 15 minutes, this non-stop shuttle service runs 100-mile-per-hour trains between London Paddington Station and Heathrow Airport, transporting 17,000 passengers daily since 1998. Fourteen Class 332 electric multiple unit vehicles operate on the line, offering passengers airline quality amenities, including telephone, screen displays and television programs, as well as lavatory and luggage facilities. Development of the line required new infrastructure, advanced technology rolling stock, and the launch of an entirely new railway company. As engineering consultant and project manager for the new company, Interfleet's responsibilities spanned the entire duration of the project, and continue in the form of engineering support of ongoing operations. Early responsibilities focused on the technical specification of the rolling stock, and related business planning. Interfleet was also responsible for finalizing all infrastructure improvements, track access agreements, operational procedures, and marketing plans for the new line. Interfleet managed the rolling stock procurement process, including evaluating manufacturers' offers and recommending a preferred supplier. Interfleet's consultancy role continued during management of the design and regulatory approval processes. With Interfleet's assistance, Heathrow Express became the first train to successfully complete the new safety and approvals process implemented following rail privatization in the UK. The Heathrow Express rolling stock has proven itself to be some of the most reliable in operation in the UK, and vehicles of the same type have subsequently been deployed by other commuter rail operations.

Above and left: Midland Metro light rail.

Below: Birmingham Metro stop.

Photography: Rail Images.

This nearly 13-mile-long light-rail route from Birmingham to Wolverhampton, with 23 stops, opened in the summer of 1999. A fleet of 16 vehicles carry up to 152 passengers each at a maximum speed of nearly 50 miles per hour along the route every eight minutes during peak operating hours. Some 5.1 million passengers traveled the line in 2003, which has increased ridership ten percent annually since opening. To improve vehicle and overall system reliability, Altram, the consortium responsible for light rail services in the West Midlands, invited Interfleet to undertake a wide-ranging strategic review of line performance. The study resulted in a reliability improvement strategy for train vehicles and the line's electrical and mechanical systems, including several recommendations for improving journey times. The firm reviewed and redesigned maintenance regimes and wrote new maintenance documentation for the entire system. The strategic review covered specific systems and problems, recommending improvements for ticket machines, passenger information systems at stops, vehicle doors and signaling systems. As part of its services, the firm studied and managed wheel-wear issues and also managed heavy repair work to vehicles and the rebuilding of a damaged vehicle, including sourcing missing parts.

Interfleet Technology

Amtrak HHP-8 Locomotive
Maintenance Support
Northeast Corridor, USA

Above: Amtrak HHP-8 locomotive.

Photography: Interfleet.

As part of the 2000 launch of the Acela high-speed train service on the heavily traveled Northeast Corridor, Amtrak also introduced a fleet of high-horsepower electric locomotives, the HHP-8, to haul conventional passenger rolling stock alongside the new Acela trains. With the approach of the HHP-8 fleet's first general overhaul, Amtrak turned to Interfleet for assistance maintaining them and improving maintenance training and documentation. The firm observed the dismantling of an HHP-8 truck and evaluated maintenance issues. Interfleet recommended changes in overall maintenance strategy to reflect international best practices. Interfleet's specialists then recommended improvements to Amtrak's tooling and maintenance facilities. Amtrak subsequently retained the firm to evaluate current test procedures and to produce a model to predict suspension behavior under test loads. The firm recommended changes to Amtrak's maintenance documents should a truck fail any test step. Amtrak reports these changes in overhaul and maintenance procedures have significantly improved the HHP-8 fleet's operations.

Interfleet Technology

ScotRail Turbostar
Procurement Plan Management
Scotland, United Kingdom

ScotRail needed to increase the frequency of its over-crowded flagship shuttle service between Edinburgh and Glasgow and to replace its aging train fleet operating in suburban Glasgow. The rail line retained a consultant team including Interfleet to develop a fast-track procurement process to acquire fleets of both diesel and electric multiple-unit vehicles. The team started by defining a procurement strategy and project plan to maximize competition among suppliers, fulfill European Union procurement and legislative requirements and meet strict timeframes. To reduce risk, the team recommended the procurement of off-the-shelf products proven in operation elsewhere in the UK. The advisory team proposed an innovative and time-saving procurement strategy of appointing the new trains' financier prior to choosing a manufacturer.

The team evaluated responses to the invitation to tender and, within two weeks of its return, had concluded agreements with lessors for both fleets. Working closely with the lessors, the consultants supported ScotRail in its negotiations with bidding vehicle manufacturers. Contracts for the fleets were concluded with Bombardier in record time, meeting all regulatory requirements, and with excellent commercial terms. Just five months passed from initial engagement of the consulting team to signing of the contracts. The first of the chosen vehicles, the 100-mile-per-hour Bombardier Class 170 'Turbostar,' fitted out to the highest standards, began operations in late 2000.

Right: ScotRail Turbostar trains.

Below: Glasgow Queen Street Station.

Bottom right: New train fleet

Bottom left: Bombardier Turbostar in operation.

Photography: Rail Images.

Singapore Mass Rapid Transit
Maintenance Audit
Singapore

Singapore Mass Rapid Transit (SMRT) engaged Interfleet to benchmark systems and workforce performance in maintaining its rolling stock, rail lines and signaling systems. SMRT's 106 electric multiple unit vehicle trains operate on 56 route miles serving 51 street-level, above- and below-ground stations and three maintenance depots. The SMRT network serves more than a million passengers daily in the major high-density travel corridors of Singapore. Interfleet carried out a strategic audit of maintenance systems and workforce quality for the entire SMRT system, benchmarking performance against comparable operations in Hong Kong, Australia and Europe. The audit covered such vital functional issues as train service delivery, clarity of maintenance communications, staff training and performance, effectiveness of maintenance review processes, implementation of changes in maintenance service and adequacy of maintenance facilities. Interfleet also made recommendations for possible future system maintenance programs.

Above: SMRT electric multiple-unit vehicles.

Below: SMRT north east line vehicle.

Below right: Train interior.

Photography: Interfleet.

LTK Engineering Services

100 West Butler Avenue
Ambler, PA 19002
215.542.0700
215.542.7676 (Fax)
www.LTK.com

LTK
Engineering Services

Above: New York City Transit R143 car.

Below left: Port Authority Trans-Hudson Corporation (PATH) Rapid Transit car.

Below right: Long Island Rail Road M-1 car in service.

Bottom right: M-7 car on the test track.

LTK has been an innovator and leader in the design and procurement of transit rolling stock and systems since its founding in 1921. The firm has participated in the design, construction, overhaul and repair of more than 12,000 passenger rail vehicles and has expertise in maintenance facilities, signals and communications, traction electrification and fare collection. In the Eastern U.S., the firm has advised most major rail transit agencies. It has played an integral role in New York City Transit's procurement of four new car fleets since 1996. Firm experts are leading the effort by PATH to upgrade its train fleet and signal system. Since 1967, LTK has advised the Long Island Rail Road, Metro-

North Railroad and the Connecticut Department of Transportation in procuring every M-Series electric multiple unit. The firm is providing similar services to New Jersey Transit for its purchase of multi-level cars and to the MBTA in its procurement of rapid transit cars for the Blue Line. Since 1991, LTK has served the Southeastern Pennsylvania Transportation Authority (SEPTA) as its on-call vehicle consultant. The firm is currently assisting Charlotte Area Transit System with the procurement of new light rail vehicles.

Above: New Jersey Transit Arrow III car.

Above right: : Delaware River Port Authority/PATCO Rapid Transit car.

Below: Southeastern Pennsylvania Transportation Authority (SEPTA) M-4 cars.

Photography: LTK.

Above and top right: Minneapolis Metro Transit Hiawatha Light Rail opening day.

Below: Chicago Transit Authority (CTA) Congress-Dearborn Subway Line.

Right: Houston MetroRail Light Rail car.

Photography: LTK.

Among its many projects in the Central U.S., LTK has assisted in design and development of the $675 million Hiawatha Corridor Light Rail project, the first LRT system in Minnesota, which opened in 2004. The firm designed all system elements, including vehicles, signals, traction electrification, communications and central control, system wide electrical, fare collection and the yard and shop. LTK served as designer and construction manager for the Chicago Transit Authority on the Congress-Dearborn Subway resignaling project. The firm has supported the Northern Indiana Commuter Transportation District for more than two decades, advising on two separate railcar procurements and a fleet overhaul. For the 7.5-mile Houston MetroRail LRT system, LTK provided the design and manufacturing review of the vehicles, signals, communications, control center and fare-collection equipment. The firm's experts have provided Dallas Area Rapid Transit (DART) with program management services and engineering support for its light rail vehicles since 1990. In addition, LTK planned and helped start up the Trinity Commuter Railway Express.

LTK
Engineering Services

Numerous cities in the West have developed new rail transit systems in recent years, turning to LTK for its vehicle and systems expertise. No agency is better equipped to assess LTK's systems engineering skills than TriMet, the Tri-County Metropolitan Transportation District of Oregon. The firm has worked with TriMet for more than two decades cov-

ering seven major projects, creating a transit system that has won international acclaim. For the Denver Regional Transportation District, LTK had responsibility for operational systems for the 1.6-mile downtown/terminal extension and the new 19-mile T-REX LRT Line. In 1994, the firm planned a range of multimodal, multi-destination transit system

alternatives for the Puget Sound area's Sound Transit, integrating light rail and commuter rail with existing bus and ferry systems. Results include the Central Link, a 14-mile LRT corridor, and the 1.6-mile Tacoma Link streetcar line. When Sacramento began to develop a LRT system, it relied on the firm's expertise in a variety of ways from procurement to

Above: Tri-Met Low-Floor Light Rail car.

Below: Sound Transit Seattle/Tacoma Link Streetcar.

Facing page: The Portland Streetcar.

Above: Los Angeles County MTA Red Line car.

Below: Denver RTD Southwest Line.

Photography: LTK.

testing of ticket vending equipment. LTK has been behind the scenes of the Los Angeles area's growing rail system for nearly two decades. The firm helped procure cars for the Red, Blue and Green Lines and is currently assisting with a car procurement for the Gold Line. LTK has also played key roles in the Southern California Regional Rail Authority's commuter rail service since its inception more than a decade ago. In San Diego, the firm has responsibility for engineering and procurement of new DMUs for the start-up commuter rail service linking several communities in the region.

Manuel Padron & Associates

1175 Peachtree Street, NE
Suite 414
Atlanta, GA 30361
404.873.3206
404.888.0418 (Fax)
mpadron@mpamundo.com
www.mpamundo.com

Manuel Padron & Associates   Atlanta Area Projects

Top right: MARTA Rail map.

Above: Trains at North Springs station.

Right: Bus-Rail Transfer Area at Arts Center station.

Below: Peachtree Center station and train.

Photography: Manuel Padron.

The Metropolitan Atlanta Rapid Transit Authority (MARTA) has engaged the firm for numerous projects over the past years. Current projects include planning for four extensions to MARTA's integrated rail and bus network, which currently serves 500,000 passengers daily. The projects include the West, I-20 East and North corridors, an arterial bus rapid transit corridor and the Beltline/C-Loop. The firm's responsibilities include planning bus and rail operations, estimating operating costs, coordinating financial planning and assisting with technology assessment and alternative evaluations. The firm previously set up a new bus system for suburban Cobb County. That system now operates 60 buses over 13 express and local routes, interfacing with MARTA rapid transit stations. Following the firm's feasibility study, neighboring Gwinnett County started up a bus system which the firm planned and implemented. Other recent projects include consulting for the Georgia Regional Transportation Authority (GRTA) on the Regional Transit Action Plan to expand transit service throughout the Atlanta region, and the operations and financial planning for two major bus rapid transit projects.

Manuel Padron & Associates   Dallas Area Projects

Above: DART Rail System map.

Left: DART train in downtown Dallas mall.

Below: Union Station aerial view showing light rail & commuter trains.

Photography: Manuel Padron.

As part of the Dallas Area Rapid Transit (DART) General Planning Consultant team, the firm prepared rail operating plans and costs analysis, including fleet size, train routings and service frequencies, for the 11.3-mile Northeast Light Rail Transit Line (to Garland). The firm also reviewed and recommended changes to DART's feeder bus plan for the initial LRT system. Among recent projects, the Northwest Corridor Study, for which the firm prepared operating plans and cost estimates, resulted in approval of two new LRT lines: the Northwest LRT Line from downtown Dallas to Carrollton and the Northwest Irving/Dallas-Fort Worth line from the Carrollton Line's Northwest Highway Station to Dallas-Fort Worth Airport. The firm also provided operating plans, cost estimates and preliminary engineering services for the 10.2-mile-long Southeast Corridor LRT line from Pearl Street in the Dallas Central Business District to the Buckner Road Station. By 2025, daily ridership on this line is expected to reach nearly 20,000.

Left: Rapid Transit District (RTD) train in downtown.

Below: RTD map.

Below left: RTD train at station.

Photography: Smith Myung.

The firm helped develop an alternatives analysis and environmental impact statement for the Southwest Corridor light rail transit line, an 8.7-mile extension of the Central Corridor line. The firm also provided bus and rail operations planning, transit-demand estimates, boarding and parking analyses and cost estimates for the project. For the congested, high-growth Southeast Corridor, the firm evaluated highway and transit alternatives. A multi-modal approach was selected, for which the firm provided bus operations plans, cost estimates and a rail operations and maintenance plan

including train scheduling. The LRT portion consists of 19.1 miles of rail service with 13 stations. As part of the planning for several other transit projects proposed in the Regional Transportation District's FasTracks program, the firm helped evaluate solutions for the 12.1-mile West Corridor LRT; the US Route 36 bus rapid transit and commuter rail corridor; the Denver I-70 multi-modal East Corridor; the Denver I-25 North Corridor Commuter Rail Project; and the I-225 LRT Line, which branches off the Southeast line now under construction.

Manuel Padron & Associates

Los Angeles Area Projects

The firm has been involved in numerous transit projects in Los Angeles for more than two decades as operations consultant to the Metropolitan Transit Authority and its predecessor agencies. The firm has conducted multiple planning studies for the Los Angeles County rail system, leading to the completion of 73 miles of rail lines with 62 stations. For those studies, the firm prepared a variety of analyses; they included ridership estimates, rail operating plans, feeder bus plans, operations cost estimates, train simulations, estimates of vehicle require-ments, schematic track plans, maintenance yard and shop function definitions and storage requirements. The firm also participated in project management oversight and the start-up of the Blue and Red lines, including contract audits, preparation of staffing plans and budgeting for operations and mainte-nance. Among other projects, the firm assisted in preliminary engineering and environmental impact state-ments for bus and light rail rapid transit lines in West Los Angeles, the San Fernando Valley and East Los Angeles.

Top: MetroRail map.

Above: Blue Line train.

Left: Metro Center Red Line station.

Below left: Aviation Station on Green Line.

Below right: Chinatown Station on Pasadena Gold Line.

Photography: Manuel Padron.

Manuel Padron & Associates   San Diego Area Projects

Among several area projects, the firm worked on the preliminary engineering and environmental impact statement for the Bayside Trolley Line. The Bayside Line connects the Trolley Line from downtown San Diego to the Mexican border and the East Line to Santee. The firm developed operating plans, ridership estimates and operations and maintenance costs for the interconnected system, as well as for a longer range planned system which is being built in stages. The Bayside Line itself added four stations to the Trolley system. The firm also prepared operating plans and estimated bus and rail operating and maintenance costs for the San Diego Mid-Coast Corridor. The work also included a financial analysis to determine the feasibility of extending the Trolley system in this corridor. A similar study analyzed the Mission Valley Trolley extension.

Top left: Bayside Trolley Line aerial view.

Top right: Bayside Line Imperial station.

Above: San Diego Trolley System map.

Left: Bayside Line America Plaza statoion.

Photography: Manuel Padron.

Manuel Padron & Associates   San Francisco Bay Area Projects

Among many Bay Area projects, the firm served as rail operations consultant or supported preliminary engineering on several BART extensions or proposed extensions. These include Concord to the Pittsburg-Bay Point station, the Dublin extension, the Colma Station and a proposed 16-mile extension to Milpitas, San Jose and Santa Clara. For the San Francisco Municipal Railway (Muni), the firm prepared an operations and cost effectiveness analysis of the proposed underground Muni turnaround. Subsequently, the firm served as operations consultant in the study of the Muni Third Street Light Rail Project in the Bayshore Corridor. Among other Bay Area projects, the firm developed an operations and maintenance cost model for the transfer of the Capitol Corridor Passenger Rail Service from the State of California to a partnership among six local transit agencies. The firm has also undertaken operations planning for extensions of the Tasman East and West light rail lines in Santa Clara County. Other recent projects include support of the preliminary engineering design of the Vasona Light Rail project, a 6.8-mile line from downtown San Jose to Los Gatos.

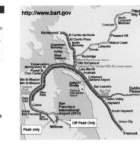
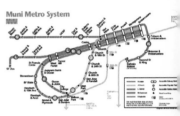

Above and right: Bay Area transit maps.

Below left: Santa Clara County Light Rail Transit.

Below and bottom right: San Francisco Muni train and station.

Bottom left: BART West Oakland station.

Photography: Manuel Padron, Dennis Markham.

Manuel Padron & Associates   Seattle Area Projects

As part of the Sound Move plan, Sound Transit implemented a network of 20 regional express bus routes connecting major sub-centers of the tri-county Puget Sound region. The firm prepared the operations plan for the network, estimated ridership, fare revenue and operating costs, and developed a financial analysis and service implementation plan. The express bus system comprises 200 buses of various lengths, which use alternative fuels, all outfitted for commuter service. The network has a daily ridership of 27,000. The firm also provided operations planning for Seattle's initial 24-mile light rail system. This system will run from north to south through the existing bus tunnel in downtown Seattle. The first 14 miles of the system, from Seattle to Tukwila, are now under construction. To ensure adequacy of the initial phase, the firm prepared an operating plan for a long-range program to extend the LRT system over a network more than 150 miles.

Above: Electric/diesel bus in Seattle.

Below: Bus in downtown tunnel.

Below right: Sound Transit network map.

Photography: Manuel Padron.

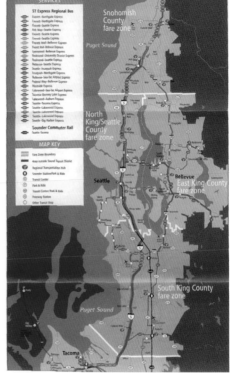

Motor Coach Industries, Inc.

1700 East Golf Road
Schaumburg, IL 60173
(866) MCICOACH (624.2622) Toll-free
(847) 285.2000 Phone
(847) 285.2013 Fax
www.mcicoach.com

Motor Coach Industries, Inc.   Product Evolution

Now the leading manufacturer of intercity coaches in the U.S. and Canada, Motor Coach Industries (MCI) traces its heritage to a small Winnipeg, Manitoba, Canada, auto body repair shop where the company built its first coach, an 11-passenger bus, in 1933. In 1939, the company designed and manufactured a new transit-type coach with the windshield over the radiator. In 1969, MCI produced the first 40-foot coach. Today, the MCI commuter coach is widely recognized for its smooth, quiet ride, forward-facing reclining seats, a generous 29 inches of legroom, overhead reading lights, individual airflow controls and other amenities. MCI commuter coaches are based on the 57 forward-facing seat capacity of the MCI D4500 and the 49-seat MCI D4000, both of which feature a specially designed, easy-to-use wheelchair lift. A stainless-steel frame helps make the MCI commuter coach extremely durable. The high-mounted radiator and charge-air cooler deter road splash and simplify maintenance. An electrical multiplexed system provides simple, accurate and time-saving diagnostics. Inside, the MCI commuter coach offers an ergonomically designed driver's compartment and a dash area with plenty of room for fare collection access.

Motor Coach Industries, Inc.   D4500, E4500 and J4500 Coaches

Early in its history, MCI became the leading coach builder for long-haul tour and charter transit lines and continues to lead the industry in overall sales. In 2003, the D4500 became the best-selling bus of all time, with more than 6,000 models sold. The D4500 cruiser coach has been serving commuter transit lines in New Jersey, New York, California, Utah and elsewhere. In 2000, New Jersey Transit awarded MCI the largest-ever transit agency bus contract, for delivery of up to 1,370 D4500 coaches. The luxury E4500 cruiser, developed for tour travel, features the industry's best payload and baggage capacities along with many innovative passenger amenities and operating advantages. MCI's luxurious E4500 was designed in association with BMW Design Works and features a spiral entryway. Football commentator John Madden travels more than 80,000 miles annually in his E4500 cruiser, his fourth MCI coach. Its sibling, the J4500, launched in 2001, has become the best-selling tour and charter coach in North America.

MCI coaches have been widely adapted for specialized uses, from luxury motor homes—most famously John Madden's E4500—to specialized service vehicles for military and police purposes. The G4500 has been built for Greyhound for many of its long-haul routes. D-Series coaches serve the U.S. Army, Air Force, Navy, Marines, INS, Border Patrol, Department of Energy and other government agencies. MCI also supplies many county, state and federal prisons with a D-based Inmate Security Transportation Vehicle, designed as a secure and safe prison on wheels. MCI also developed four hybrid-drive coaches for New Jersey Transit. The hybrid coaches use diesel fuel and regenerated energy for propulsion power, featuring the Allison EP 50 electric-drive hybrid propulsion system. New Jersey Transit operates 76 CNG MCI commuter coaches as well.

Above: New Jersey Transit hybrid-drive commuter coach.

Below: Inmate Security Transportation Vehicle.

Above: Greyhound G4500.

Right: D4500 commuter coach.

Below: Roaring Fork. Transportation Authority (Aspen, Colorado) commuter coach.

Below right: Commuter coach wheelchair lift.

Photography: MCI.

Over its 70-year history, MCI has won numerous awards for technology, design, and engineering. Innovation remains a company hallmark. In recent years, the company has expanded its Winnipeg plant and re-engineered its state-of-the-art mixed-model assembly line. Marking a clean-technology and fuel-reduction milestone, the company delivered four hybrid diesel-electric commuter coaches to New Jersey Transit. The expanded online ordering capabilities, the Louisville, KY, parts facility and a national network of Fleet Support Service Centers help ensure little downtime for repair and maintenance.

Above: NFL broadcaster John Madden and his MCI E4500.

Below left: MCI Fleet support parts and technical assistance.

Below: New Jersey Transit MCI commuter coach

Photography: MCI.

New Flyer

711 Kernaghan Avenue
Winnipeg, MB R2C 3T4
Canada
888.222.6968 (Toll Free)
204.224.1251
204.224.4214 (Fax)
www.newflyer.com

New Flyer

New Flyer

Hybrid Transit Buses
Seattle, Honolulu, Albuquerque, Hartford,
Orange County, California, and elsewhere

Left: DE60LF.

Below: DE40LF, photo courtesy of *BUSRide* Magazine.

Photography: New Flyer.

New Flyer, the leading manufacturer of heavy duty urban transit buses in North America, offers the industry's widest selection of hybrid-electric transit vehicles, with diesel-electric and gasoline-electric hybrid buses in 30, 35, 40, and 60-foot lengths. New Flyer hybrids are operating in metropolitan areas from Orange County, CA, to Hartford, CT, with many more orders on hand. The recently introduced 60-foot, articulating DE60LF seats 64 passengers with room for an additional 55 standees. The bus is configured as a normal diesel propelled bus, with a CAT C9

optimal RPM. As the brakes are applied, energy captured from the brakes (regenerative braking) charges the rooftop batteries. A thorough road-test by King County Metro of Seattle, Washington, showed that, in addition to reductions of up to 90 percent of airborne emissions, major savings in diesel fuel (750,000 fewer gallons and half a million dollars annually in the Seattle area) and maintenance costs (mechanical components and brake linings) will be realized immediately. In September, 2003, Seattle's King County Metro and Sound Transit placed the largest hybrid-

engine and an Allison E^{V}50 electric drive system. As the bus accelerates from a stop, energy from the batteries stored on the roof provides the required propulsion. At higher speeds, the engine provides assistance at an

electric transit bus order ever, for 235 DE60LF units, as a result of successful testing earlier that year.

New Flyer

D40i (Invero™)
Burlington, Ontario; Everett, Washington; London, Ontario; Ottawa, Ontario; St. Catharines, Ontario; Winnipeg, Manitoba

Above: D40i (Invero).

The Invero™, a 40-foot, low-floor, diesel-powered transit vehicle, provides panoramic windows and comfortable seating for up to 44 passengers, with an additional 46 standees. The low-floor design, kneeling feature and two-stage flip-out wheelchair ramp make it completely ADA compliant. Structural features include fiberglass, corrosion-resistant side panels, removable, dent-resistant lower skirt panels and advanced bumper technology. The forward roof-mounted HVAC system distributes weight evenly for better handling. The panoramic windows, 26 percent larger than on comparable buses, isolate noise, and reduce dust and water intrusion, lowering maintenance costs. An advanced lighting system reduces window glare. New Flyer, the leading manufacturer of low-floor buses in North America, delivered its first Invero in 2002. Since then, several transit agencies in the U.S. and Canada have made fleet purchases, including a 290-vehicle order by Ottawa's OC Transpo. A 60-foot, articulating, diesel-electric hybrid version of the Invero is now being engineered by the company. The bus will enable transit agencies to switch to lower-emission and reduced-fuel fleets without needing to invest in new fueling facilities.

Above: D40i (Invero).

Right: DE60i (Invero).

Below: No-glare, panoramic windows on D40i (Invero).

Photography: New Flyer.

New Flyer began bus manufacturing in 1930 and has been responsible for many innovations since. The company introduced the "low-floor" bus to the North American market in 1988 and today has more than 12,000 in service, leading the industry in units sold and in revenue service miles. Low-floor buses come in 30-, 35-, 40-, and 60-foot articulated models. With large doors, no steps, anti-slip flooring and generous aisle width, New Flyer buses are safe and convenient. A seat-level large window design improves riders' visibility.

New Flyer was the industry's first manufacturer to supply Programmable Logic Controllers (PLC) in production buses as standard equipment. PLC enables multiplexing with only one wire raceway, simplifying electrical systems. New Flyer's heavy-duty monocoque frame is constructed with high tensile steel plate and tube welded to produce a durable shell. For maintenance crews, the company's combination of training, electronic manuals, and customer service makes their tasks easier and less time consuming. The commonality

Below: D60LF.

Photography: New Flyer.

of parts between different models helps reduce operating costs. The many transit agencies currently operating New Flyer low-floor buses include Connecticut Transit (Hartford, CT), SEPTA (Philadelphia, PA), Metropolitan Transit Authority (Houston, TX), Capital Metro (Austin, TX), Utah Transit Authority, Salt Lake City, UT), Tri-Met (Portland, OR), Sound Transit (Seattle, WA), King County (Seattle, WA), Omnitrans (San Bernardino, CA), and Orange County (CA) Transportation Authority.

North American Bus Industries, Inc.

20350 Ventura Blvd.
Suite 205
Woodland Hills, CA 91364
818.610.0330
818.610.0335 (Fax)
www.nabiusa.com

North American Bus Industries, Inc.

Models 35-LFW, 40-LFW, 60-LFW Low-Floor Buses, Models 416, 436 Standard-Floor Buses
Los Angeles, Chicago, Denver, Boston, Miami-Dade, Oakland, Arlington Heights, Phoenix, Cleveland

Above: 40-LFW buses in Los Angeles.

Bottom: World-class engineers on two continents.

The sole business of North American Bus Industries (NABI) is the sale, assembly and post-delivery support of a full range of transit buses. The company focuses on simplicity of use in its products and innovative, practical, flexible solutions to the urban problems of sustainability and livability. This approach has helped NABI emerge as the third largest supplier of transit buses in the United States. Many municipalities have chosen the company's low-floor and standard-floor buses in lengths of 35, 40 and 60 feet (articulated). Seating can be customized in suburban, transit or perimeter arrangements, with capacity ranging from 30 to 62 seats. The heavy-duty buses are manufactured out of stainless or mild steel in a two-step process: the shells are made in Hungary and final assembly is completed in Alabama with American mechanical components in compliance with "Buy America" regulations. Among a wide range of options, all buses are available with a choice of power train, including ultra-low-sulfur diesel and compressed or liquefied natural gas.

Above: Chicago Model 60-LFW.

Right: NABI 40-LFWs in LA's Metro Rapid BRT system.

Photography: NABI, LA Metro.

North American Bus Industries, Inc.

Model 30-LFN, Shuttle Bus
Miami-Dade Transit, American Eagle Airlines

Above: Forward axle model 30-LFN.

Right: Ultra low-floor convenient for passenger boarding/alighting.

Below: Powered fold-out ramp.

Bottom: Wide doorway.

A shuttle bus should provide passenger comfort and safety, assure long-term economical operation and look sharp year after year. With more than 1,500 vehicles currently on the road worldwide, Optare's Solo—called the Model 30-LFN in the U.S.—has won two prestigious British awards for styling. Constructed of easily maintained stainless steel and corrosion-resistant aluminum, the bus comes in either a single-door model offering 31 cushioned seats or a two-door configuration seating 26 passengers. The large, clear, slide-glide entrance door permits easy entry and egress while the ultra-low, kneeling floors and powered fold-out ramp simplify boarding. The axle

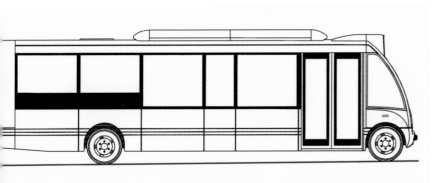

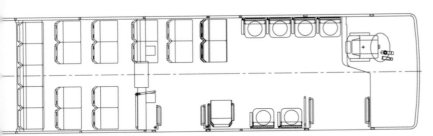

Above: Room for two wheel-chairs.

Left: Elevation drawings and seat layout for the award-winning 30-LFN.

Below: Miami-Dade Transit.

Photography: NABI.

in both door configurations sits forward of the front door, eliminating the forward passenger area wheel-housing and providing excellent wheelchair maneuverability and comfort. At a best-in-class 7.5 miles to the gallon, the cradle-mounted, low-emissions diesel engine, in combination with the 5-speed automatic transmission, provides a 27 percent improvement in fuel-economy over the nearest competitor, based on 12-year lifecycle, government-required Altoona testing data.

North American Bus Industries, Inc.

Model 40C-LFW, 45C-LFW CompoBus® Transit Buses
Phoenix, Los Angeles, Chicago, Tempe, Lancaster

Above: Phoenix RAPID CompoBus® service.

Right: Low-floor wheelchair ramp.

Far right, top to bottom: Perfect for BRT applications; Model 40C-LFW CompoBus®; regular route seating; commuter-express interior.

Near right: Unitized composite-resin chassis and body form a completely corrosion resistant, durable composite "shell."

Photography: NABI, LA Metro.

Ridership in the Phoenix bus system jumped 65,000 passengers annually following introduction of its new RAPID line with a fleet of 56 CompoBuses. The aerodynamic-style buses have large windows, attractive interior finishes, reading lights, luggage lofts and refrigeration vents for each of the 41 high-back, padded seats. NABI utilizes a patented high-vacuum, resin-transfer technique to produce large, single-piece composite structures of unusually high consistency and quality. The crash-resistant unibody shell of glass- and carbon-fiber reinforced, vinyl-ester resin laminate significantly reduces weight, simplifies repair, and completely resists corrosion. The lightweight, unitized composite structure allows the use of lower-power, lower-emission engines and advanced propulsion systems without sacrificing performance. This combination of lighter weight and reduced power significantly reduces fuel costs. The structure's lighter weight also extends brake life and reduces tire wear. Moreover, with none of the rust and corrosion of aging conventional buses and greater crash resistance, the costs of preventive maintenance and body and structure repairs fall sharply.

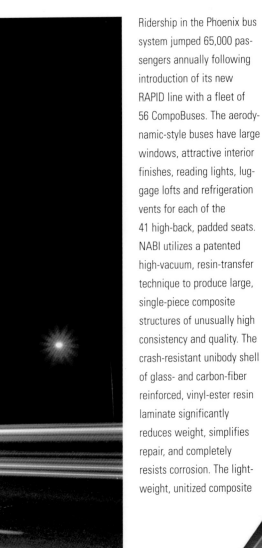

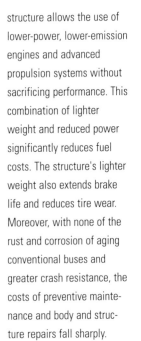

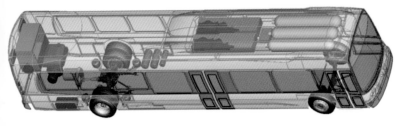

North American Bus Industries, Inc.

Model 60-BRT Articulating Bus
Los Angeles

With its swooped windshield, aerodynamic-style side mirrors and rail-like design, this high-capacity, articulated bus is changing the paradigm of bus rapid transit—enabling operators to increase passenger capacity and appeal. These advances led the Los Angeles County Metropolitan Transportation Authority to order 200 of the buses, with an option for 400 more. The 60-foot, low-floor, bellows-linked double bus can seat up to 60 passengers in a variety of available seating arrangements and styles. Constructed of stainless steel, the bus features diesel or alternate fuels engine, fully cradle-mounted for easier removal or installation. Befitting its high tech look, the bus offers automatic passenger counter, stop announcement and vehicle monitoring systems.

Left: Production of the pilot 60-BRT bus.
Below: 60-BRT.

Otak, Inc.

117 S Main Street
Suite 400
Seattle, WA 98104
206.224.7221
206.224.9230 (Fax)

10230 NE Points Drive
Suite 400
Kirkland, WA 98033
425.822.4446
425.827.9577 (Fax)

36 N Fourth Street
Carbondale, CO 81623
970.963.1971
970.963.1622 (Fax)

Corporate Office

17355 SW Boones Ferry Road
Lake Oswego, OR 97035
503.635.3618
503.635.5395 (Fax)

www.otak.com

700 Washington Street
Suite 401
Vancouver, WA 98660
360.737.9613
360.737.9651 (Fax)

1345 NW Wall Street
Suite 100
Bend, OR 97701
541.385.9960
541.312.8704 (Fax)

435 NW Fifth Street
Suite D
Corvallis, OR 97330
541.738.1611
541.738.1612 (Fax)

51 W Third Street
Suite 201
Tempe, AZ 85281
480.557.6670
480.557.6506 (Fax)

Otak, Inc.

Tacoma Link Light Rail Transit Line
Tacoma, Washington

The first contemporary light rail project constructed in the Puget Sound region, the 1.6-mile Link LRT Line connects major cultural destinations in downtown to the intermodal transportation center at Freighthouse Square in the Tacoma Dome District. The firm led a multidisciplinary team of 15 consultants to complete final engineering, design and construction services, bringing construction documents to bid within one percent of the cost estimate. The line's five stations and canopies were designed as a "family of stations" to facilitate system identity, but with integrated art and landscape reflecting the character and history of the surrounding neighborhood. The project included a maintenance facility for Sound Transit, utility relocation, underground areaway and significant street reconstruction, intersection design and design support services during construction. Other improvements along the route included new sidewalks, pedestrian lighting, street trees, benches, community kiosks and changes to side streets to improve pedestrian access to the stations. The Tacoma LRT is already exceeding ridership projected for the year 2010.

All: "Family of stations."

Top left: Theater district station.

Left: Station canopy artwork.

Below left: Station platform artwork.

Right: Tacoma light rail station at Freighthouse Square.

Below: Art in landscaped median at Union Station.

Photography: Art Grice.

Otak, Inc.

Tacoma Dome Commuter Rail Station
Tacoma, Washington

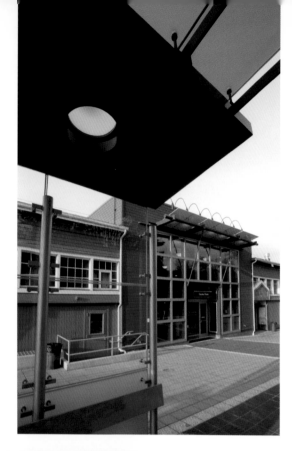

Left: Commuter rail canopy.

Right: Concourse and access.

Below: Platform.

Bottom: Sound Transit commuter rail train.

Opposite page: Concourse.

Photography: Art Grice.

This station currently serves as the terminus of the Sounder Commuter Rail line and is at Tacoma's intermodal hub. The firm provided architecture, civil engineering and urban planning services to create a new 2,000-square-foot concourse inserted into the historic Freighthouse Square building. The project also required construction of an at-grade platform with canopies and windscreens. The concourse now serves as the focal point of the Station, connecting the train platform with recently completed intermodal facilities that include a park-and-ride garage, commuter buses, the Link LRT station and a nearby Amtrak station, and the surrounding downtown neighborhood. Soon after opening, 2,000 commuters per day were passing through the station.

Otak, Inc.

Central Phoenix/East Valley Light Rail Transit
Phoenix, Tempe and Mesa, Arizona

Left: Light rail station and transit center at Sun Devil Stadium, Tempe.

Below: Cooling Screen louvers.

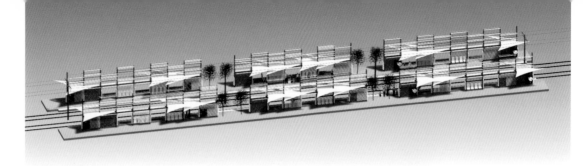

The Valley's light rail system will offer riders a speedy link between the cities of Phoenix, Tempe and Mesa and will be an integral part of a comprehensive Valley-wide transit system. The 20.3-mile starter segment will include up to 28 stations, several park-and-ride facilities and three bus transit centers serving the light rail stations and key destinations. The project has been divided into five line sections for design and construction, with four in Phoenix and the fifth in Tempe/Mesa. Within each line section a different architectural team is responsible for the design of the stations. While Otak's team is primarily responsible for the station architecture in Tempe/Mesa, the team's Cooling Screen concept for tempering southern Arizona's blistering heat on station platforms was chosen for all 28 stations. The Cooling Screens arrange a series of large-scale louvers and fabric canopies for maximum shading for any site location and sun-angle direction. This approach offers a solution to the extreme environmental conditions and also creates a distinctive system identity while allowing each station to connect to its regional architecture and art through site-specific elements.

Above: Cool Screen concept.

Left: University Drive and Rural Road Station.

Below left: Third Street and Mill Station.

Bottom left: University Drive and Rural Road Station rendering.

Below: Station art concepts by: below, Suikang Zhao; center, Dan Carson and bottom, Christine Bourdette.

Images: Otak + Architekton.

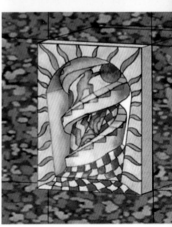

151

PARSONS

WMATA
Washington, DC

Left: WMATA, King Street station, Alexandria, VA.

Below: WMATA, Virginia Square station, Arlington, VA.

Since 1966, Parsons has served the Washington Metropolitan Area Transit Authority (WMATA) as General Engineering Consultant for the Washington, DC metropolitan region's 103-mile, $9.7 billion rail rapid transit system. Facilities include 84 stations and intermodal transfer terminals, commuter car parks for 30,000 autos and 48 miles of subway, including 22 miles of cut-and-cover tunnels, 14 miles of earth tunnel and 15 miles of rock tunnel. A significant portion of the transit system was built within heavily developed commercial and residential areas. The firm's role has included preliminary engineering design of the entire system, planning, route location, property requirements, budget estimates, right-of-way design criteria, preliminary and final right-of-way plans, surveying, property maps, overall design criteria, design standards and specifications. In addition, the firm managed the design of aerial, at-grade and subway structures; trackwork; traction power; train control and communications; yards and shops; system safety evaluation; noise and vibration control; and maintenance procedures. Parsons also coordinates the ongoing design for the automatic train control system, providing automatic train protection, operations and supervision

Above: WMATA, trains and landmarks, Washington, DC.

Below left: WMATA, Ronald Reagan Washington National Airport.

Below right: WMATA, Gallery Place station, Washington, DC.

Photography: WMATA.

PARSONS

Transportation Expansion Project (T-REX)
Southeast Corridor Light Rail Transit Extension
Metropolitan Denver, Colorado

As part of a design/build joint venture with Peter Kiewit & Sons, Parsons is the lead engineer for the design and construction of the Transportation Expansion Project (T-REX), a five-year design-build contract that is adding a light rail transit service extension and improving 17 miles of highway through the southeast Denver metropolitan area. T-REX is the largest transportation project undertaken in Colorado history and is the result of a unique collaboration between the Regional Transportation District, the Federal Transit Administration, the Colorado Department of Transportation, and the Federal Highway Administration. T-REX final design and construction began in fall 2001. Construction is scheduled for completion in September 2006 with light rail planned for start-up of revenue service in late 2006. Parsons is the primary designer for the 19 miles of double-track

Top: T-REX light rail system expansion rendering.

Above: Work on T-REX system along highway.

light rail transit along I-25 and I-225. The transit service includes 13 new transit stations, 12 park-n-ride lots, three new parking structures, a new operations control center, power and signal systems, and a supervisory control and data acquisition system for the existing transit lines. Parsons is testing the 34 light rail vehicles that are being added to RTD's fleet to service this corridor.

Above: Construction of elevated light rail.

Below: T-REX station under construction.

Photography: Colorado Department of Transportation.

Rendering: Parsons.

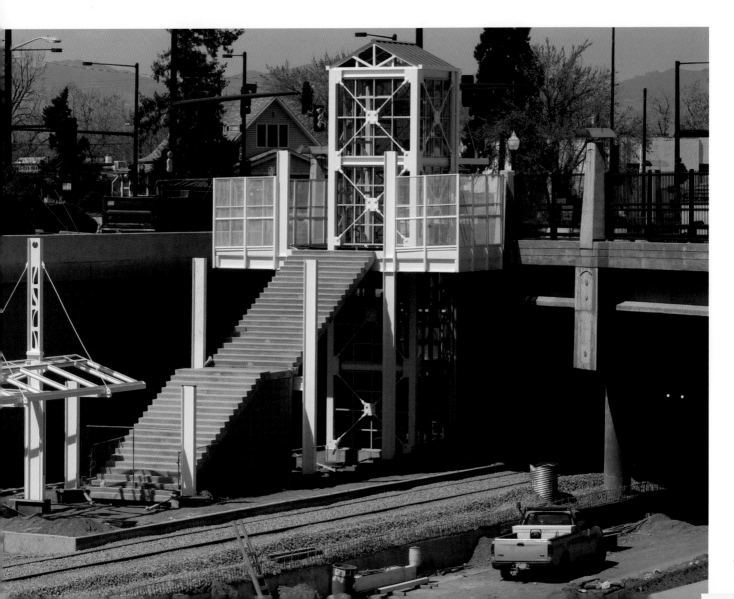

MBTA Operations Control Center
Boston, Massachusetts

As prime consultant to the Massachusetts Bay Transportation Authority (MBTA), Parsons oversaw the design and installation of its new Operations Control Center (OCC) for rapid transit, light rail and surface bus operations and the extension from five to ten stories and complete renovation of a downtown Boston building for the center. The OCC is housed in a column-free, theater-style facility with a mezzanine for an operations briefing and supervisory room, emergency control and a conference room, with a view of the overall display board. The OCC design included supervisory control and data acquisition for infrastructure and traction power control; voice communications by radio and telephone; and centralized traffic control and automatic vehicle identification for surveillance and control of rail traffic. The project provides operations personnel with real-time information and identification of atypical conditions. The project required development of interfaces to new and existing systems and their presentation to operators as an integrated working environment at 42 work stations and on an overview display wall. The firm also designed and managed installation of a new two-way radio system network through which all departments will be able to talk directly to each other and emergency assistance personnel. The new OCC has allowed the MBTA to perform all control functions while reducing operations personnel by nearly half.

Above: Work stations and wall display.

Left: MBTA Operations Control Center.

Below: Real-time system data and images.

Photography: Parsons.

PARSONS

Charlotte South Corridor Light Rail Project
Charlotte, North Carolina

The firm serves as the prime consultant for the engineering, environmental and investment studies, design and construction management for this 9.6-mile, double-track light rail line and its 15 stations along a diverse urban corridor. Planning needed to assure that future development in station areas meets the overall city planning objective of focusing development within the corridors served by major transit investment. The line will require construction of 1.3 miles of bridge structures for trains and pedestrians and the development of pedestrian walkways along the tracks. The line will pass through the city's convention center building and a hotel in the central business district. The fast-tracked design schedule required coordination with the recently built Charlotte Trolley, which will share tracks with the light rail service for 3.5 miles.

Above: Elevated station; (Rendering by: Sasaki & Associates).

Below left: Light rail vehicle; (Rendering by: Siemens Transportation).

Below right: Light rail bridge over major thoroughfare; (Rendering by: Parsons).

RNL Design

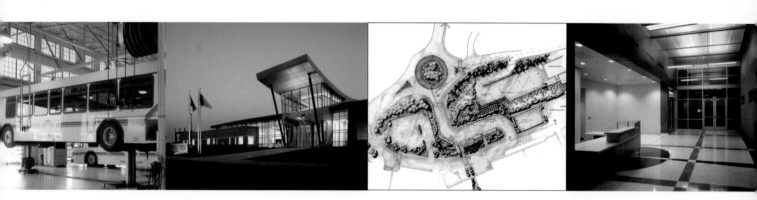

1515 Arapahoe Street
Tower Three, Suite 700
Denver, CO 80202
303.295.1717
303.295.0845 (Fax)

800 Wilshire Boulevard
Suite 400
Los Angeles, CA 90017
213.955.9775
213.955.9885 (Fax)

4450 North 12th Street
Suite 260
Phoenix, AZ 85014
602.212.1044
602.212.0964 (Fax)

www.rnldesign.com

RNL Design

Foothill Transit Irwindale Operations & Maintenance Facility
Irwindale, California

Foothill Transit serves the local and regional bus transportation needs of the small communities extending eastward from Los Angeles along the San Gabriel Mountain range. The new center provides facilities to manage, park, clean, fuel and maintain 156 buses from the agency's 300-bus fleet, with the capacity to service all compressed natural gas (CNG)-fueled vehicles as the fleet switches over from diesel to the CNG fuel-standard, so important to regional air quality. The RNL team previously designed Foothill Transit's original

Maintenance and Operations Facility in Pomona and worked closely with Foothill Transit to develop a state-of-the-art facility. Built on the precipice of a two-mile wide rock quarry, the new facility faces away from the partially water-filled depression and projects the community face of the administration building to the adjacent regional-connecting roadway. Service-bay doors and other employee spaces were positioned in a way that shields them from strong sunlight and continual prevailing winds. Reflecting local Spanish-hacienda and mission-farm

traditions, the facility is reminiscent of Spanish Mission architecture, with a stucco exterior, metal roof tiles, a trellised concourse and complementary interior elements.

Left: Interior corridor.

Below left: Mission style administrative entrance.

Below: Service bays.

Facing page: Trellised concourse.

Photography: Derek Rath.

The Elati Maintenance Facility serves as the center of all daily maintenance operations for the fast-growing Regional Transportation District (RTD) light rail transit (LRT) system. The largest LRT facility in the U.S., the 125,000-square-foot building provides facilities for administration, operations, maintenance, maintenance-of-way and storage of up to 100 vehicles. The 110,000-square-foot maintenance portion of the facility has 18 bays, including a wash/service bay, wheel-truing lathe bay, ten recessed maintenance pits, five additional repair bays, parts storage area, an electronics shop and other system repair service areas. Other facilities include administrative office and meeting space, lunch rooms and locker rooms. Ladder tracks allow trains to be parked overnight or driven directly through the nine high-bay doors, which open on both the north and south sides for speedy roll-through. The building's vaulted standing-seam metal roof soars over the entire facility, with a sweeping, glass-enclosed main entryway thrusting out toward the street entrance. RNL Design, which provided architectural and interior design services, faced the building's exterior with brick and stone-masonry veneer and a translucent wall system near the top of the arched 55-foot roof. The natural daylight in the maintenance area enhances the work environment and reduces the costs of artificial lighting. Part of an urban renewal area, the facility and a planned neighboring LRT station should act as a catalyst for further local development.

Above: Maintenance facilities.

Left: Entrance and administrative areas.

Below: Night-time view.

Photography: Ed LaCasse.

RNL Design

Old Town Transit Center
Park City, Utah

Park City is a popular jumping off point for the ski slopes used as major sites for the 2002 Olympic Winter Games. Built in anticipation of the influx of visitors for the Olympics, the center serves as a transfer point where buses, taxis and private vehicles bringing people to Park City can interchange with buses taking skiers to the nearby slopes and pedestrian access to the town. The center offers facilities for ticketing, boarding and waiting as well as a drivers' break room and a maintenance area. A new

intermodal roundabout replaced a dangerous three-way intersection, improving bus access to the center from adjacent streets. Site work created a new bicycle trail and tunnel, a new stream bed and a parking lot. As design architect for the project, RNL Design responded sensitively to Park City's historical and topographical contexts. On the site of a demolished silver ore mill in an historic district, the center's bus driveway retaining wall was constructed in part from the mill's original stone foundation walls. The

pitched metal roof with high windows and interior use of heavy timber roof structure tied with steel tension rods in a king post system are reminiscent of the historic mill. Sited on a sloping street, the two-story building allows access from two different levels.

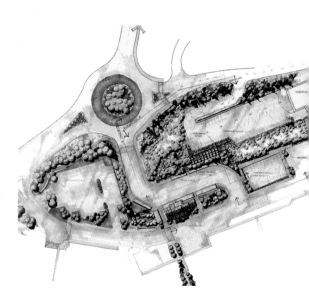

Above: Interior with heavy timber construction.

Top: Site plan.

Facing page top: Boarding area.

Right: Two-level access.

Photography: Michael Moore.

Above: Maintenance building.

Left: Administrative building entrance.

Below: Administrative building interior.

Photography: Jim Christy and Mark Boisclair.

With continued unprecedented growth in the Phoenix-Mesa region, the City of Mesa expects to expand its bus fleet to over 200 buses in the next few years. RNL Design provided Mesa with the program, master plan and design for a two-phase facility to accommodate a 100-bus fleet in the initial phase with future expansion to 200 buses, plus a planned park-and-ride facility. The project team developed a landscaped campus of buildings using a palette of materials appropriate to the Southwest desert environment. Similar materials, detailing and massing give coherence to the composition and provide a standard for future development. The first-phase facility provides 21,000 square feet for administrative and operational functions and 54,500 square feet for maintenance functions. A two-wing administrative building provides a street presence for public access, with large canopies to shade glazed facades. The maintenance building complements the administrative center by being divided into two distinct masses, one housing maintenance bays and the other parts and support functions.

Sasaki Associates, Inc.

64 Pleasant Street
Watertown, MA 02472
617.926.3300
617.924.2748 (Fax)
info@sasaki.com
www.sasaki.com

900 North Point Street
Suite B300
San Francisco, CA 94109
415.776.7272
415.202.8970 (Fax)
sanfrancisco@sasaki.com

Sasaki Associates, Inc.

Dallas Area Rapid Transit Mall
Dallas, Texas

Above: Transitway Mall aerial view.

Above right: Station during evening hours.

Below: Station markers identify stations.

Below right: Public art at station.

Facing page: Transitway Mall station and open-space corridor.

Photography: Greg Hursley.

This mile-long transitway mall along the DART light rail transit line corridor links several districts with the downtown core and forms a major open-space system. The entire length of the mall is unified with street trees, special streetscape treatments and a public arts pro-gram. Station markers desig-nate the location of each of the four transit stations in the mall, while the design of the blocks between the sta-tions serves to distinguish the transitway, local vehicu-lar access and pedestrian zones. These streetscape improvements support the development of retail uses, an increase in streetlife and a safer environment during off-peak hours. As the prime consultant for the award-winning project, the firm pro-vided project management, urban design and landscape architecture services. An interdisciplinary design approach with many profes-sional firms and an innova-tive construction phasing plan minimized any adverse impacts on local merchants. Working with local and national artists enhanced the quality of the environment.

Sasaki Associates, Inc.

San Francisco Waterfront Transportation Projects
San Francisco, California

Left: Muni MMX N-line.
Below: N-line shelter.

The firm provided urban design, planning, and landscape architecture services for a variety of transportation projects along the city's waterfront. For the 2.5-mile Embarcadero Waterfront Roadway, the scope encompassed design review of all streetscape elements, coordination of public art projects and recommendations for street furnishings. The firm also implemented a review process that estab-

Above: South Embarcadero.

Above right: Light rail trackway.

Right: Embarcadero streetscape.

Photography: Patrick Carney and Sasaki Associates.

lished a set of design principles for evaluating future design decisions. For the new Municipal Railway (Muni) MMX N-line along the South Embarcadero, the firm led the urban design team in identifying the design goals and coordinating with the public and private stakeholders. The team created transparent glass-roofed shelters with a sinuous form, originally conceived by the artist Anna Murch, that alludes to the shapes of the waves in the bay and distant hills. The light rail trackway was marked by cobbles to distinguish it from surrounding pedestrian zones. In addition, the firm developed and implemented the shelter design for the historic F-line streetcar transit line on the North Embarcadero.

Sasaki Associates, Inc.

Cleveland Waterfront Transit Line
Cleveland, Ohio

The 1.5-mile-long Waterfront Transit Line connects to the existing Red, Green and Blue lines. Beginning at Tower City, it proceeds west along the Red Line tracks, then runs north through the "Flats" entertainment district along the Cuyahoga River before swinging east along the Lake Erie waterfront. It passes near the new Cleveland Browns football stadium, the Rock and Roll Hall of Fame and other attractions, before ending at the South Harbor station, a short distance east of East Ninth Street. On a fast-track schedule for completion during Cleveland's 1996 bicentennial, the extension improved access for workers, shoppers and visitors to the city's growing cultural and entertainment attractions and reduced traffic congestion. Serving as urban designer, landscape architect, graphic designer and traffic engineer, the firm worked to create a cohesive image for the new line and to integrate stations, bridges, trackway, streetscape and other components into the surrounding city. Each station features white latticework structures and glass canopies. At each station an artist produced integrated elements, such as railings, wind chimes, paving or lighting. Parsons Brinckerhoff served as prime consultant for the project.

Above left: Station area directional signage.

Above right: White latticework and glass canopy at station.

Left and right: Settlers Landing Station aerial view.

Below: Station along Lake Erie.

Photography: Alex MacLean/ Landslides, Bill Schuemann, Sasaki Associates.

Sasaki Associates, Inc.

Euclid Avenue Bus Rapid Transit Corridor
Cleveland, Ohio

The firm and its associates were called upon to create a boulevard corridor with an exclusive center median busway running adjacent to automobile traffic along the 5.5-mile Euclid Avenue Corridor. The busway will connect the central business district with the University Circle area and major cultural, medical and educational districts. The corridor encompasses eight different neighborhoods with buildings of varying sizes and scales. The route will have 63 stations, with streetscape improve- ments designed to encourage transit and bike usage, including new sidewalks, passenger shelters at stops, pedestrian lighting, street trees and tree lawns. The shelters' distinctively angled roof and glass walls will provide system identity and weather protection for riders waiting to board buses. Modifications to roadways and traffic regulations will enhance the experience along the transit corridor. Wilbur Smith Associates acted as prime consultant.

Top: Euclid Avenue with busway stops and exclusive bus lanes.

Right and left above and below: Euclid Avenue corridor before and after.

Photography and Rendering: Sasaki Associates.

Siemens Transportation Systems, Inc.

7464 French Road
Sacramento, CA 95828
916.681.3000
916.681.3006 (Fax)
www.sts.siemens.com

Siemens Transportation Systems, Inc.

New York City Transit Rail Automation
New York City

New Yorkers will soon realize a longstanding desire: waiting at subway platforms without checking their watches or peering down the tracks in search of the next train. Interpreting muffled announcements on outdated loudspeakers will also be a thing of the past. Siemens technology will allow riders to view train arrivals and departures on screens and to listen to crisp messages on a new public address system. Part of the same upgrade, dispatchers will no longer need to alert conductors about train breakdowns with walkie-talkies. Instead, a central hub will pick up this information, help reroute trains and reduce congestion. As joint-venture consortium leader, Siemens has four contracts to upgrade and automate core parts of the subway communication and control operation—the Automated Train Supervision Center, the ATM Sonet, the Communication-Based Train Control System and the Public Address/Customer Information system. New York's century-old subway system is the fifth largest in the world with 1.3 billion riders annually. Implementing the latest technology on its infrastructure that spans 800 miles and operates around-the-clock represents a major challenge. Siemens responded with integrated solutions centered on a state-of-the-art control station that provides a continuous communication link with the city's 468 stations. The firm installed a fiber optic network called ATM Sonet, which upgrades the communications system that links each station and sends information to the central command station. The new carrier-grade system will increase bandwidth capabilities of the current system and allow transmission of voice and data with synchronous optical network (Sonet) and asynchronous transfer mode (ATM) technologies. The ATS command center, the nucleus of all four projects, is located in a theater-like center the size of a football field. When complete, it will be the largest and most complex such operation in the world. The Communication-Based Train Control (CBTC) system uses electric commands instead of physical signals to control and reroute trains. This technology will improve safety and increase the number of trains running on existing infrastructure. The Public Address/Customer Information System (PA/CIS) will allow passengers to watch train traffic on screens, listen to live voice announcements and change travel plans accordingly.

Top: Customer information screen system.

Above: New York Subway automatic train supervision control center.

Left: Real-time train information display.

Right: Integrated public address-customer information screen system.

Photography: Siemens Transportation Systems.

Siemens Transportation Systems, Inc.

MAX Light Rail Vehicles and Electrification
Portland, Oregon

Above: MAX light rail vehicle in downtown Portland.

Right: MAX traction power sub-station.

Far right and below: MAX light rail vehicles and overhead catenary.

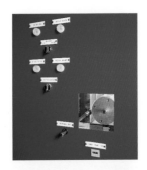

Top, above and left: Signaling and telecommunications infrastructure.

Photography: Siemens Transportation Systems.

Siemens has been responsible for the design, manufacture, installation, testing and commissioning of light rail vehicles and traction electrification systems serving most of Portland's TriMet's Metropolitan Area Express (MAX) 44-mile light rail system. The firm has served on three major MAX projects, the Westside Extension, Airport MAX and Interstate MAX Extension. Siemens' delivered a total of 52 low-floor, bi-directional, six-axle, articulated light rail vehicles for the MAX Westside Extension and Airport MAX lines. The vehicles were the first low-floor light rail cars to be used in revenue service in the United States; now they are the standard for new LRV purchases across the country. The vehicles have a passenger capacity of 64 seated, four spaces for wheelchairs, four bicycle racks and room for 204 standees. TriMet has 27 additional light rail vehicles on order from Siemens, with 17 currently in revenue service. These newest vehicles are essentially the same as those already in service, except they have automatic passenger counters, a different air conditioning system and new paint scheme. For the three MAX extension projects, the firm supplied the light rail traction electrification system. This comprised a total of 31 traction power substations and 32 miles of overhead catenary, as well as signaling, telecommunications and street lighting components.

Siemens Transportation Systems, Inc.

METRORail
Houston, Texas

Houston's first light rail line, the METRORail Red Line, a $324 million, 7.5-mile route with 16 stations connecting downtown Houston with the southern portion of the city, began service in early 2004. It operates along the Main Street corridor, a key artery linking Downtown Houston to Midtown, the Third Ward, the Texas Medical Center, three major universities, the Museum District, Hermann Park and the Zoo, and the growing Reliant Park, which now includes a new football stadium, exhibition center and other venues. METRORail is projected to spur $500 million to $1 billion in economic development along its path, and its annual boardings are estimated at 10 million to 13 million by 2020, or about 40,000 boardings each weekday. Siemens worked with contract partners to build, design and install the light rail vehicles, systems for communications, supervisory control and data acquisition (SCADA) and signaling. The firm also was responsible for ticket vending, civil work, track work and traction power supply, traction power distribution

Facing page: METRORail station.

Above left: Extra-wide door.

Above: Downtown operations.

Below left: Main Street corridor.

Below: S70 light rail vehicle.

and overhead catenary systems. Siemens supplied 18 S70-type vehicles. Each is 95 feet long with seating for 72 passengers; seated and standing capacity is 200 people. In the future, as ridership increases, cars can be linked up to a two-car train to carry 400 passengers. Each car is low-floor for 70 percent of its length. The ends of the vehicles are elevated to allow full performance running gear and car-body strength. Each car has four extra-wide doors per side in the low-floor section for ease and speed of boarding and complete accessibility. Plans call for extension of the line another five and one-half miles from the current end of the line at the University of Houston/ Downtown northward to Northline Mall, and include five new stations.

Above: Communications system.

Below: Station, light rail vehicle and overhead catenary.

Below right: Supervisory control and data acquisition workstation.

Photography: Siemens Transportation Systems.

Silvester + Tafuro, Inc.

50 Washington Street
South Norwalk, CT 06854
203.866.9221
203.838.2436 (Fax)
www.silvestertafuro.com
j_silvester@silvestertafuro.com

Silvester + Tafuro, Inc.

Silvester + Tafuro, Inc.

Retail Shops in Train Stations
Hudson News at Grand Central Terminal
New York, New York

Left: Hudson News entrance from restored terminal passage.

Below left: Newsstand interior.

Bottom: Curvilinear forms in walls, ceiling and floor.

Photography: Peter Paige.

Hudson News is the client's flagship, transit-facility retail outlet, offering regional, national, and international magazine titles, newspapers and books, along with snacks and beverages, health & beauty aids, tobacco products, souvenir apparel and regional gifts. This outlet's location, in a bustling passageway restored as part of the revival of the landmark Grand Central Terminal, makes it one of the most prominent and busiest newsstands in the nation. During peak hours, it serves some 60 clients per minute. With openings to passageways on three sides, the site presented particular challenges for creating sufficient merchandising space for more than

3,000 titles and easy circulation for customers. To use all possible floor space, systems for the facility are hidden within the ceiling. A central cashier and display area speeds customer checkout. Curved display racks with three-sided extensions maximize wall space. Curvilinear forms are also used for signage and in the recessed central overhead lighting system, which also displays a 25-foot-diameter LED news-ticker. The pattern of the poured terrazzo floor repeats the curved walls. The same rich sapele veneer casework found in the shelving walls and racks is used for trimwork throughout the shop.

Silvester + Tafuro, Inc.

Amtrak Auto Train Superliner Conversion
Sanford, Florida

Above: Dining car upper level.

Rendering: Rick Roseman.

Amtrak's Auto Train runs nonstop from Lorton, Virginia — just south of Washington, DC — to Sanford, Florida. The existing two-level dining cars were functionally outmoded and required complete rebuilding. The rebuilt cars are expected to last 20 years under heavy usage, despite limited maintenance resources. The cars needed to provide two floors of dining, bar service and restrooms as well as a smoking section and television lounge. The firm's design concept created a completely new floor plan for the two levels joined by an enhanced staircase. The upper level features forest green vinyl with beige piping radial booth seating at half-round tables on one side of the car and a single line of two-seat tables on the other. Each row is broken by a centrally located bar service and condiment station. Lighting tubes recessed into the beige, textured-laminate wall panels and ceiling lights designed to respond to vibration from rail travel keep the space bright and lend it a larger appearance. The lower level has a similar layout, with smoking and television lounges. "Upon completion food and beverage sales increased 70% within the first six months of operation," said John McCaffrey, Amtrak's Auto Train project manager.

Silvester + Tafuro, Inc.

Retail Shops in Terminals
d-parture spa
Newark Liberty Airport, New Jersey

Left: Destination entry and signage.

Below left: Curvilinear glass walls.

Photography: Peter Paige.

Right: Interior spaces.

Below: Newark Airport Terminal C d-parture spa.

Photography: Peter Paige.

Trips with limited legroom and recycled air, lengthy layovers and delays make terminal-based spas an appealing option for travel-weary passengers. Located in two storefronts in Newark Airport's Terminals B and C, d-parture spa offers quick-service spa treatments along with a line of travel-ready treatment and cosmetic products. The d-parture spa brand is defined through its store design, visual merchandising, graphic design, content and service. The designers developed a dramatic entry combined with a sophisticated electronically modulating sign to create a recognizable destination within the busy concourse. Curvilinear glass and white walls and forms attract passersby and delineate the interior's spaces, storage and product displays. Suspended glass shelves highlight products while a soothing palette of light natural wood, clear glass, white walls and mint-green accents establish the calm of a spa experience within a vibrant, congested travel facility.

Silvester + Tafuro, Inc.

Retail Shops in Terminals
Passport Travel Spa
Indianapolis International Airport, Indiana

Passport Travel Spa's 834-square-foot facility is located near the airport's busy food court. The outlet, the first of several being planned, offers a full range of professional spa services to air travelers and airport personnel, including nail care, hair styling and massage. The firm provided full design and architecture services, including branding to create a flagship-store identity. The award-winning logo and materials share soothing tones of grey, green, and blue. Working with a limited budget and abbreviated time frame, the firm had to design a facility around the existing in-line space with nine-foot ceilings. The perimeter walls were covered with slat wall to ensure maximum flexibility for the start-up operation. Glass shelving provides retail space for product sales. Suspended hoops with fabric membranes obscure and diffuse existing fluorescent lighting and create focal elements just below the existing ceiling plane. Sliding glass doors with obscure glass at the rear of the facility provide storage areas.

Above: Terminal spa entry.

Right: Suspended fabric membrane.

Facing page: Logos and spa products.

Photography: Peter Paige.

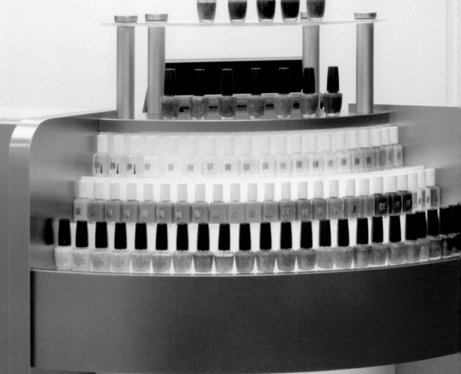

Silvester + Tafuro, Inc.

**Retail Shops in Terminals
Sprint PCS**
Central Terminal, LaGuardia Airport, New York

The firm needed to create a retail outlet in a busy terminal that conveyed the client's corporate commitment to premium communications products. A prototype facility, it needed to reinforce the brand identity of the firm while maintaining flexibility and components to accommodate future installations. The entire brand statement is conveyed through four materials: a neutral wood flooring, red laminate walls, clear-glass display cases and shelving and aluminum trim and panels. The centrally located retail display case with light well above centers the store and serves to create the symmetrical layout display for retail display and circulation. Cable-suspended light boxes and cases make replacing advertising material simple. All stations are lit from indirect coves above. Ceiling-mounted wall-washers focus on the credenza units. The cases are lit internally and from below, helping to convey the quality and contemporary nature of the product offerings.

Above: Display cases and cable-suspended light boxes.

Right: Terminal store entry.

Photography: Peter Paige.

Stacy and Witbeck, Inc.

1320 Harbor Bay Parkway
Suite 240
Alameda, CA 94546
510.748.1870
510.748.1205 (Fax)
www.stacywitbeck.com

Stacy and Witbeck, Inc.

Interstate MAX Light Rail Yellow Line Extension
Portland, Oregon

Left: Evening view.

Right top: Interstate/Rose Quarter north view.

Right center: MAX Yellow Line.

Right bottom: Track-bed construction.

Opposite page: Interstate/Rose Quarter south view.

Photography: Bruce Forster.

The Interstate Metropolitan Area Express (MAX) project extended Portland's MAX Yellow Line 4.7 miles northward from the Rose Quarter Arena along the center median of Interstate Avenue through North Portland neighborhoods to the Metropolitan Exposition Center. The firm served as general contractor for the project, which was completed six months ahead of schedule without cost overruns. It was the first to use the Construction Manager/ General Contractor delivery system for a federally funded light rail extension and is now considered a model for the process. Extending the line involved laying ballasted and paved double track, constructing eight platforms, relocating utilities, widening and reconstructing streets, developing park-and-ride facilities and installing artwork. Virtually every business and residence along the construction corridor was affected, requiring close coordination with the community stakeholders. This project proved "painless construction" could be accomplished on time and under budget. Among the line's many complex components, the team built a four-span, cast-in-place bridge over the primary rail access to the Union Pacific Railroad's intermodal yard without disrupting train movement.

Stacy and Witbeck, Inc.

Mid-Embarcadero Surface Roadway and F-Line Extension
San Francisco, California

Above: Embarcadero Promenade.

Left: Fisherman's Wharf.

Center left: Streetcar stop.

Bottom: Landscaping Embarcadero Promenade.

Opposite page: Embarcadero Promenade aerial view.

Photography: Susan Lohwasser.

San Franciscans long desired a direct streetcar link between Downtown and Fisherman's Wharf. That vision was realized with completion of Muni's F-Market and Wharves historic streetcar line. Before the extension, the line, which begins at Castro and Market Streets, ended at the Transbay Terminal. In 1988, Stacy and Witbeck began the first phase of the Market Street F-Line Extension and went on to complete all five phases on the Market Street work and then the Embarcadero section in the 1990s. The 2.5-mile line now travels along the Northern Waterfront to Fisherman's Wharf and Pier 39. As the general contractor, the firm built the new trackway, including canopied stops, and totally reconstructed the roadway, signals and utilities without disrupting traffic for the 10 million annual visitors to Fisherman's Wharf, the city's most popular tourist destination. Part of the project included creation of a major urban plaza, the Embarcadero Promenade. Honoring the firm's role in the project's success, the Mayor of San Francisco officially proclaimed June 16, 2000, as Stacy and Witbeck, Inc., Day.

Stacy and Witbeck, Inc.

University and Medical Center Light Rail Transit Line Extensions
Salt Lake City, Utah

In the first of this project's two phases, the design-build team constructed the first 2.5 miles of the TRAX University Line from downtown Salt Lake City to the University of Utah's Rice-Eccles Stadium. Roadway and light rail construction on a main downtown artery proceeded round-the-clock to complete work in time for the 2002 Olympic Winter Games. Nonetheless, the project caused minimal business and community disruption, as UTA and the design-build team implemented numerous public outreach efforts to communicate construction plans and progress. The firm served as a member of a joint-venture general contractor team responsible for the design and reconstruction of hundreds of old underground utilities, roadway widening and construction of miles of new curb, gutter and sidewalk. The team also designed and built concrete trackway and stations, laid double rail lines and constructed an overhead catenary system and three traction power substations. Also included were 15 miles of pavement reconstruction and a public arts program. The entire line was lit and landscaped—with specialized plantings to minimize water usage—creating a boulevard look. The same

Above: Opening day.

Right: Heavy university campus ridership.

Left: University Line.

198

team was selected to build the 1.5-mile extension of the Line to the University's Health Sciences Center. This phase included two center and one side platform stations, a single and a double crossover, plus roadway and utility work. Now complete, the TRAX University Line project has won more than ten major awards including the Associated General Contractors Marvin M. Black Excellence in Partnering 2004, Aon Build America Award 2004 and Design-Build Institute of America Transportation Project 2003 honors. The four-mile Line currently carries more than 10,000 riders each weekday.

Top: Trackway construction.

Above: Winter public transit to University.

Above: Winter public transit.

Right: New boulevard and rail line.

Sumitomo Corporation of America

600 Third Avenue
New York, NY 10016
212.207.0700
212.207.0845 (Fax)
transit@sumitomocorp.com
www.sumitomocorp.com

Sumitomo Corporation of America   Commuter Rail Electric Multiple Units
Chicago; Indiana

In 2002, Sumitomo (SCOA) and its partner and rail car manufacturer, Nippon Sharyo, celebrated their 20th anniversary of supplying commuter rail cars in the United States. In that time, the partners have delivered more than 450 rail transit cars to Chicago Metropolitan Rail (Metra), the Northern Indiana Commuter Transportation District, the Maryland Transit Administration, California CALTRANS Peninsula Corridor Joint Powers Board, the Los Angeles County MTA and the New York City Transit Authority. SCOA's partner also holds the largest market share of Japanese "Shinkansen" bullet train sets. The partnership is supplying 26 new Highliner EMU (electric multiple unit) cars for Metra. The gallery, or bi-level, EMU cars will operate exclusively on Metra's Electric District, which serves nearly 45,000 passengers each weekday on the 31-mile route between Chicago's Randolph Street Station and University Park. The Highliner EMU car has a stainless steel body fully compliant with all transportation-related regulations and structural requirements. The state-of-the-art AC propulsion system with individual motorized axles has been proven reliable in North American service. Its Train Information Management System (TIMS) provides real-time information tracking location and expected time of arrivals onboard and at stations. Wheelchair lifts are located at all passenger entrances and every car has a wheelchair-accessible toilet.

Left: Rendering of new Metra Highliner EMU.

Above: Chicago South Shore Line Electric Multiple Unit (EMU).

Photography, Rendering: Nippon Sharyo.

Sumitomo Corporation of America

Gallery-Type Bi-Level Commuter Rail Push-Pull
Passenger Car
Chicago; Bay Area, California

SCOA was the recipient of a $398-million procurement order for commuter rail cars, the largest ever in Illinois history and one of the largest ever in the commuter railroad industry. Metra, the Northeast Illinois commuter rail system based in Chicago, named SCOA in association with Nippon Sharyo as its supplier for 300 new stainless steel gallery-type bi-level commuter cars. Under Metra's "Build Illinois" provision, SCOA is allocating a portion of the contract value to manufacturers and suppliers from within the state. The new gallery cars will replace more than one-third of Metra's old locomotive hauling coaches. Each Gallery Car seats approximately 150 riders, nearly triple a standard transit car, significantly increasing potential ridership per train. CalTrain provides commuter rail service between San Francisco and Gilroy along the San Francisco Peninsula and also utilizes SCOA's push-pull bi-level gallery cars.

Above: Caltrain gallery type bi-level commuter rail car.

Left: Metra gallery type bi-level commuter rail car.

Photography: Nippon Sharyo.

Sumitomo Corporation of America

Articulated Light Rail Vehicle
Los Angeles, California

Above: Metro Blue Line light rail vehicle.

Photography: Nippon Sharyo.

Sumitomo supplied the Los Angeles County MTA with the 54 light rail vehicles running on the region's first light rail system, the 22-mile Metro Blue Line between Los Angeles and Long Beach, which opened in 1990. Five years later, the firm delivered 15 identical vehicles for the 20-mile Metro Green Line operating between Norwalk and Redondo Beach. Each line operates its fleet of articulated, six-axle,

double-ended, pantograph-powered vehicles. The Green Line fleet light rail vehicles run in two-car trains at speeds up to 65 miles per hour for its daily ridership of more than 23,000. The Blue Line fleet operates in three-car trains at up to 55 miles per hour to carry an average of more than 63,000 passengers each day. The trains can accelerate from 0 to 55 miles per hour in 45 seconds. Each vehicle can seat 150 riders,

with a maximum capacity of 230 seated and standing riders plus two wheelchairs. The cars carry such conveniences as air conditioning, a security intercom system, seating for handicapped, and floors level with station platforms for ease of boarding.

Sumitomo Corporation of America

Crystal Mover Automated People Mover System
Miami; Washington, DC; Singapore, Incheon, Korea

Above: Singapore Crystal Mover automated people mover system.

Right: Dulles International Airport Crystal Mover interior rendering.

Facing page bottom: Crystal Mover on guideway.

In partnership with Mitsubishi Heavy Industries, Sumitomo has supplied and has been constructing several state-of-the-art automated people mover (APM) systems in the USA. The same systems can also be seen in Singapore and Korea. With its crystal-cut design and distinctive color scheme, the team's Crystal Mover APM projects an ultramodern image. The computer-controlled Crystal Mover runs on rubber wheels along a guideway and is capable of speeds of up to 50 miles per hour. Each car can accommodate approximately 100 people. The high-technology interiors provide exceptional visibility, computerized passenger information displays and a smooth, comfortable ride. In Singapore, Crystal Mover is used to link railway terminal stations with the New Town. The system began public operations in December 2002. The partnership is completing the 0.7-mile APM system with 20 vehicles for Miami International Airport's new World Gateway Terminal. A similar system will be delivered and installed at the

Above: Dulles International Airport Crystal Mover with multi-car configuration.

Photography, Rendering: Mitsubishi Heavy Industries.

Washington Dulles International Airport, with an expected 2008 opening. Operating below-ground between four stations, the 29 Crystal Mover vehicles will run along a 2.1-mile, dual-lane guideway. Korea's Incheon Airport will also build a half-mile underground system to connect an existing terminal to a new concourse under construction.

PROJECT / VEHICLE CREDITS

Exceptional care has been taken to gather information from firms represented in this book and transcribe it accurately. The publisher assumes no liability for errors or omissions in the credits listed below.

ANIL VERMA ASSOCIATES, INC.

Metro Red Line Vermont/Beverly Subway Station
Client: Los Angeles County Metropolitan Transportation Authority
Principal Consultants: Anil Verma Associates, Inc. - Prime Contractor, Project Manager, Architect of Record
Subconsultants: Transit & Tunnel Consultants and Holmes & Narver
George Stone, artist

Auburn Commuter Rail Station and Transit Center
Client: Central Puget Sound Regional Transportation Agency (Sound Transit)
Principal Consultants: Anil Verma Associates, Inc. Project Managers, Architect of Record and Urban Designers

Rio Piedras and University of Puerto Rico Underground Stations, Tren Urbano
Clients: Puerto Rico Highways & Transportation Authority, Ten Urbano Office
Principal Consultants: Design/Build Team for the Rio Piedras Contract
Kiewit Construction Company, Kenny Construction Company,
H.B. Zachry Company, a Joint Venture, and CMA
The KKZ Design/Build Team
Jacobs Sverdrup, Engineering
Anil Verma Associates, Inc. - Architect of Record and Urban Designers

South Sacramento Corridor Light Rail
Client: Sacramento Regional Transit District (SRTD)
Principal Consultants: Anil Verma Associates, Inc.- a 50% Partner with Entranco (Prime) Construction Manager for the Project

North Hollywood Metro Redline, Segment III
Client: Los Angeles County Metropolitan Transportation Authority)
Principal Consultants: JMA – Construction Management Team
Anil Verma Associates, Inc. – subconsultant responsible for Tunnels and Stations

BOOZ ALLEN HAMILTON

Metro Gold Line Light Rail Transit
Client: Los Angeles to Pasadena Metro Blue Construction Authority dba Metro Gold Line Foothill Extension Construction Authority
Principal Consultants: Booz Allen Hamilton, program management
Delcan, engineering management and quality assurance
Suverdrup, construction management
Gannett Flening, project controls and financial management
Montgomery Watson, third-party coordination
Gruen, station architectures
Kaku, traffic engineering and alternative analysis

The River LINE
Client: New Jersey Transit Corporation
Principal Consultants: Booz Allen Hamilton, program management
DMJM Harris, preliminary engineering
Boswell Engineering, engineering

TransLink® Regional Fare Card Program
Client: Metropolitan Transportation Commission
Principal Consultants: Booz Allen Hamilton, program management, engineering services
Nelson Nygaard, accessibility evaluation and design
Acumen Building Enterprise, installation and testing oversight

Information Technology Renewal Program
Client: Washington Metropolitan Area Transit Authority
Principal Consultants: Booz Allen Hamilton, system integration, change management
Advanced Software Systems (Assyst), software
PeopleSoft, software
MRO, software

London Underground Improvements
Client: Tube Lines
Principal Consultant: Booz Allen Hamilton, systems engineering, technology assessment, procurement, technical specifications

CH2M HILL

West Side Transit Facility
Client: City of Albuquerque Transit Department
Principal Consultants: CH2M HILL, vehicle maintenance facility specialty planning, design and construction services
DWL Architects & Planners, Inc. of New Mexico, architecture

Aurora Avenue North Multimodal Corridor
Client: City of Shoreline, Washington
Principal Consultant: CH2M HILL, predesign study, design, engineering, environmental documentation

Central Link Light Rail
Client: Sound Transit
Principal Consultant: CH2M HILL, civil engineering final design, construction support services

I-5 High Occupancy Vehicle (HOV) Lane Widening
Client: Orange County Transportation Authority
Principal Consultant: CH2M HILL, design, engineering, construction services

Southwest Light Rail Line
Client: Regional Transportation District
Principal Consultant: CH2M HILL, environmental impact statement, planning analyses, conceptual design (of 2-mile extension)

University and Medical Center Light Rail Transit Lines
Client: Utah Transit Authority
Principal Consultants: CH2M HILL, managing partner design joint venture
SLC Rail Constructors, design-build team

DAIMLER CHRYSLER COMMERCIAL BUSES NORTH AMERICA

Orion VII
Clients: MTA New York City Transit, Toronto Transit Commission (TTC), Washington Metro Area Transit Authority (WMATA), others
Principal Consultants: Orion Bus Industries, design, manufacturing, sales, service
Cummins, diesel and CNG engines
BAE Systems, hybrid propulsion system

Setra S417
Clients: A Yankee Line, Arrow Stage Lines and Premier Coach Company, others
Principal Consultants: Setra of North America, sales and product support
EvoBus GmbH/Setra World Headquarters, design and manufacturing;
Detroit Diesel, diesel engine
Allison, transmission

SLF 200
Clients: Transit Authority of Lexington (LexTrans), Greater Cleveland Regional Transit Authority, Prince George's County (Maryland) Transit, others
Principal Consultants: DaimlerChrysler, design, manufacturing, sales, service
Mercedes-Benz, diesel engine
Cummins, diesel, CNG engine
Allison, transmission

Sprinter Shuttle
Clients: University of Toledo, Holiday Tours, Grayline-Nashville,Runways Shuttle
Principal Consultants: DaimlerChrysler, design, manufacturing, sales, service
Mercedes-Benz, diesel engine, transmission

DAVID EVANS AND ASSOCIATES, INC.

Airport MAX Light Rail Extension
Client: TriMet (Tri-County Metropolitan Transportation District of Oregon)
Principal Consultants: David Evans and Associates, Inc., design-build team prime engineer, lead designer
Bechtel Infrastructure Corporation, design-build team manager, design, construction
Design: Finley McNary Engineers, LTK Engineering Services, Siemens Transportation Systems, STV, ZGF Partnership
Construction: Bechtel, DBM, Dirt and Aggregate, Goodfellow Brothers, Mass Electric, Sigcon, Stacy and Witbeck, Tice Electric, United Switch and Signal

National Park Service Transportation System
Client: National Park Service, Denver Service Center
Principal Consultants: David Evans and Associates, Inc., team leader
Transportation systems, design, visitor management: EDAW, Manuel Padron & Associates, Lea+Elliott, Inc., John J. McMullen Associates, IBI Group, University of Vermont, Dornbusch Associates, ORCA Consulting, The Douglas Group, Levy Consultancy Group

Interstate MAX Yellow Line Extension LS10C Segment
Client: TriMet (Tri-County Metropolitan Transportation District of Oregon)
Principal Consultants: David Evans and Associates, Inc., design-build team prime engineer, design management, engineering design, survey, permitting, construction engineering
F.E. Ward, design-build contractor, construction, dirt and aggregate expansion
Tice Electric, electrical contractor
MRC Company, track construction
Geotechnical Resources, geotechnical engineering

Spokane Regional Light Rail Project
Client: Spokane Transit Authority (STA)
Principal Consultants: David Evans and Associates, Inc., project management, civil engineering, track design, traffic engineering, bridge engineering, real estate services, quality control, construction planning services
URS, design support, project clearance
LTK Engineering, system engineering
ALSC Architects, architecture
Newlands and Company, 3D animation and visual simulation
Crandall and Arambula, transit oriented development planning

DMJM HARRIS, INC.

TRI-RAIL Double Track Corridor Improvements Program
Client: South Florida Regional Transportation Authority
Principal Consultants: DMJM Harris, Inc., project management and construction management; transportation planning; facilities planning; design, engineering and quality assurance oversight; bus route planning and operational planning
PBS&J, engineering review, project controls, construction oversight
Booz | Allen | Hamilton, contract administration, signal and passenger information, system engineering review and oversight
Craven Thompson & Associates, survey, scheduling and construction oversight
PACO Group, configuration management and office management
LKG-CMC, document control and scheduling/estimating
Dickey Consulting Services, community outreach
Tierra, Inc., materials testing
Geosol, Inc., geotechnical review and materials testing
Chitester Management Systems, Inc., schedule impact analysis
SEB Associates, ADA compliance
GRL Engineers, Inc., drilled shaft cross-sectional logging oversight

Second Avenue Subway
Client: MTA Capital Construction/New York City Transit
Principal Consultants: DMJM Harris, Inc., joint venture with Arup, preliminary engineering, engineering for environmental impact statement, security system design
GZA, geotechnical services
Mueser Rutledge, geotechnical services
CTE, civil engineering
Metcalf & Eddy, environmental engineering
Naik-Prasad, civil engineering/surveying
Sam Schwartz Co., traffic engineering
Stellar Services, GIS/IT Consultant

Frank R. Lautenberg Rail Station at Secaucus Junction
Client: New Jersey Transit
Construction Management Team: DMJM Harris, Inc., joint venture with Don Todd Associates.
HNTB Corp and Architects DiGeronimo
Design Team: Edwards and Kelcey, Inc., prime design consultant
Brennan Beer Gorman/Architects, architect
Thorton-Tomasetti Engineers, building structural engineer
Arora & Associates, bridge engineers

Washington Metro
Client: Washington Metropolitan Area Transit Authority
Principal Consultants: DMJM Harris, Inc. (as part of Capital Transit Consultants, Joint Venture), project management; preliminary engineering; design-build procurement strategies; architectural, civil, structural, electrical communications and trackwork engineering; environmental services; capital program planning
PBQD, project management, preliminary engineering
PTG, preliminary engineering
Booz | Allen | Hamilton, vehicle design and procurement
Washington Group, systems engineering

Metrolink Commuter Rail System
Client: Southern California Regional Rail Authority
Principal Consultants: DMJM Harris, Inc., design engineering, program management, construction management
J.L. Patterson & Associates, Inc., track, civil and structural Engineering
Myra Frank & Associates/Jones & Stokes, environmental
Ninyo & Moore, geotechnical engineering
Earth Mechanics, Inc., geotechnical engineering
Milbor-Pita Associates, tunnel engineering
Cornerstone Studios, Inc., landscape architecture
William J. Yang & Associates, electrical and mechanical engineering
Asahi Surveying, Inc., surveying
The Culver Group, surveying
L.D. King, surveying

EDWARDS AND KELCEY

Frank R. Lautenberg Rail Station at Secaucus Junction
Client: New Jersey Transit
Principal Consultants: Edwards and Kelcey, conceptual planning, environmental assessment, and preliminary/final design
Brennan Beer and Gorman, architectural design
Thornton-Tomasetti Engineers, station structural engineer
FR Harris and Don Todd Associates, construction management

Highbridge Yard and Care Appearance Facility
Client: Metro-North Railroad
Principal Consultants: Edwards and Kelcey, lead engineer, civil and structural design, rail operations coordination, project staging
Slattery Skanska, joint venture partner, construction contractor

Hiawatha Corridor Light Rail Transit System
Client: Metro Transitways Development Board
Principal Consultants: Edwards and Kelcey, structural design bridges, walls, traction power and overall system quality
Granite Construction, contracting
C.S. McCrassan, contracting
Parsons Transportation Group, design

Lake Street Interlocking Project, Chicago Union Station
Client: The Chicago Union Station Company
Principal Consultant: Edwards and Kelcey, planning, design and construction services

23-Mile Rail Extension Project, Worcester, MA
Client: Massachusetts Bay Transportation Authority
Principal Consultant: Edwards and Kelcey, project management, coordination of design, civil engineering, traffic engineering, structural design, environmental permitting

FOX & FOWLE ARCHITECTS

Times Square Subway Station
Client: Times Square Center Associate
Principal Consultants: Fox & Fowle Architects, architecture
Atkinson Koven Feinberg, mechanical/electrical/plumbing engineering
Carlos Dobryn Consulting Engineers, structural engineers
Ann Kale Associates, lighting
Roger Whitehouse, signage
Morse Diesel, construction manager

Roosevelt Avenue Intermodal Station
Client: MTA New York City Transit
Principal Consultants: Fox & Fowle Architects, Architecture, Sustainable Design
Domenech Hicks & Krockmalnic, Assoc. Architect
Vollmer Associates, Structural / Civil
Cosentini Associates LLP, MEP
Slattery Skanska / Gottlieb Skanska, Contractor

Second Avenue Subway Line
Client: MTA/New York City Transit
Principal Consultants: Fox & Fowle Architects
DMJM Harris / Arup: civil, structural & mep

Hoboken Light Rail Station
Client: New Jersey Transit Authority
Principal Consultants: Fox & Fowle Architects
21st Century Rail Corporation, contractors
STV – civil, structural
Domingo Gonzalez. lighting
HM White Site Architects, landscape architects

Bergenline Avenue Tunnel Station
Client: New jersey Transit Authority
Principal Consultants: Fox & Fowle Architects
Zimmer Gunsul Frasca Partnership, planning
Parsons Brinkerhoff Quade Douglas: site, civil, and structural
Herb Levine Lighting Design
Wallace Roberts Todd, landscape

Newark-Elizabeth Rail Link
Client: New jersey Transit Authority
Principal Consultants: Fox & Fowle Architects
URS / Parsons Brickerhoff Quade Douglas
KS Engineers
Ann Kale Associates, Lighting

Stillwell Avenue Terminal
Client: MTA New York City Transit
Principal Consultants: Fox & Fowle Architects
Earthtech: site, civil, and structural
Ann Kale Associates, Lighting

GRUEN ASSOCIATES

Los Angeles to Pasadena Metro Gold Line
Client: Los Angeles to Pasadena Metro Blue Line Construction Authority
Principal Consultants: Gruen Associates, urban design, station architecture, landscape design, public art coordination; bid documents, public outreach for project management team
Artist Depicted: Teddy Sandoval–Paul Polubinskas, John Valdez, Judd Fine, Michael Slutz, Cheri Gaulke
Booz-Allen, prime contractor, project management tram
Engineering Management Consultant, schematic design
Kiewit/Washington, design-build contractor

Santa Monica Boulevard Transit Parkway
Client: Los Angeles County Metropolitan Transportation Authority
Principal Consultants: Gruen Associates, urban design, landscape design, planning, environmental impact services, public outreach
Meyer Mohaddes Associates, prime contractor, transportation planning and engineering
Barbara McCarren, artist
TAHA, environmental impact report
City of Los Angeles, final design documents

CenterLine Urban Rail Corridor Projects
Clients: City of Fullerton, City of Costa Mesa, Orange County Transportation Authority
Principal Consultants: Gruen Associates, urban design, land use strategy, station concept design
Sverdrup-Jacobs, prime contractor, project management and transportation planning

San Fernando Valley East-West Bus Rapid Transitway
Client: Los Angeles County Metropolitan Transportation Authority
Principal Consultants: Gruen Associates, project management, conceptual planning, urban design, conceptual station design, land use analysis, major investment study, environmental impact statement, environment impact report
Meyer Mohaddes Associates, traffic and transportation planning
Terry A. Hayes Associates, air quality analysis
Parsons Transportation, civil engineering
Manuel Padron & Associates, modeling and operating analysis
Myra L. Frank & Associates, environmental impact report services
Harris Miller Miller & Hanson, noise analysis
Consensus Planning Group, public outreach

Bus Rapid Transit Station Plan
Client: Orange County Transportation Authority
Principal Consultants: Gruen Associates, programming, planning, urban design, station design, landscape design, brand identity
Sweeney Consulting, public outreach

Grossmont Trolley Station Transit-Oriented Development Plan
Client: City of La Mesa, Community Development Department
Principal Consultants: Gruen Associates, feasibility study, master planning, urban design, conceptual architectural design, landscape design
Keyser Marston Associates, real estate advisory

HNTB CORPORATION

Big Four Depot/Riehle Plaza
Client: Lafayette Railroad Relocation
Principal Consultant: HNTB
Walsh Construction Company, general contractor
Blitch Architects, design consultant for pedestrian bridge

Charlotte 2025 Land Use/Transit Plan
Client: Charlotte MecKlenburg Planning Commission and Charlotte Department of Transportation
Principal Consultant: HNTB, urban planning services

Minneapolis-St. Paul Light Rail Transit Tunnel and Station
Client: Minneapolis-St. Paul Metropolitan Airports Commission
Principal Consultant: HNTB, tunnel design engineering, mechanical systems, construction services, geotechnical analysis, project management, fire and life safety
Obayashi Corporation, tunnel construction
Johnson Brothers, tunnel construction
Hatch Mott MacDonald, TBM tunnel design
CNA Consulting Engineers, geotechnical, underground planning
American Engineering, testing, geotechnical
Enviroscience, construction services
Hammel Green Abrahmson, Lindbergh station design

Leonard P. Zakim Bunker Hill Bridge
Client: Massachusetts Turnpike Authority
Principal Consultant: HNTB, final design consultant, engineer of record, construction phase services
Figg Bridge Engineers, subconsultant
Rowan Williams Davies & Irwin, wind consultant
Haley & Aldrich, Inc., geotechnical
R.D. Kimball, electrical and utilities
David Mintz & Associates, lighting
Bechtel/Parsons Brinckerhoff, central artery tunnel project management consultant

BART San Francisco International Airport Extension
Client: Bay Area Rapid Transit
Principal Consultant: HNTB, electrical/mechanical design, systems design, structural and civil design, trackwork design, architect of record
Tutor-Saliba/Slattery, general contractor

South Station Transportation Center
Client: Massachusetts Bay Transportation Authority
Principal Consultant: HNTB, electrical/mechanical design, systems design, structural and civil design, trackwork design, architect of record, interior design and build-out
HNTB/TAC (The Architects Collaborative), joint venture
Zaldastani Associates, structural engineering
Cosentini Associates, mechanical engineering
Mariana D. Molina, PC
Acentech, air quality
GZA GeoEnvironmental, geotechnical

HUBNER MANUFACTURING CORPORATION

Articulation Systems and Folding Bellows for Buses
Clients: New Flyer, Neoplan, NABI
Principal Consultant: Hubner, articulation system, folding bellow

Folding Bellows for Monorails
Clients: City of Seattle, Transit Systems Management
Principal Consultants: Hubner, folding bellow
Bombardier Transportation, monorail design, construction

Canopy and Bellows for Jet Gangways
Clients: Airport operators
Principal Consultants: Hubner, folding bellow, canopies
Krupp Thyssen, jet gangway design, manufacture, installation

Passageway Systems for Trains and Light Rail Vehicles
Clients: Amtrak; Metropolitan Transit Authority of Harris County, Texas (Houston METRORail); Minnesota Department of Transportation (Hiawatha Light Rail); Sacramento Regional Transit District; others
Principal Consultants: Hubner, articulation system, folding bellow
Siemens, light rail vehicle
CAF, light rail vehicle
Bombardier, train

INTERFLEET TECHNOLOGY LTD.

Heathrow Express Project Management and Engineering
Client: British Airport Authority plc (BAA plc)
Principal Consultants: Interfleet Technology, engineering, project management, rolling stock specification and acquisition, regulatory approvals, rolling stock service support
Siemens, manufacturer electric multiple unit vehicles

Midland Metro Reliability Improvement Program
Client: Altram
Principal Consultants: Interfleet Technology, strategic review, maintenance regime development
John Laing plc, track, stops, buildings construction
Ansaldo Trasporti, vehicles, signaling, communications, overhead line equipment, power supply

Amtrak HHP-8 Locomotive Maintenance Support
Client: Amtrak
Principal Consultants: Interfleet Technology, maintenance strategy review, test procedure evaluation
Bombardier-Alstom, HHP-8 electric locomotive manufacturer

ScotRail Turbostar Procurement Management
Client: National Express Group (NEG)-ScotRail
Principal Consultants: Interfleet Technology, joint venture with First Procurement Associates (FPA), procurement management
Bombardier, train manufacturer

Singapore Mass Rapid Transit Maintenance Audit
Client: Singapore MRT Ltd (SMRT)
Principal Consultant: Interfleet Technology, maintenance audit and benchmarking

LTK ENGINEERING SERVICES

Eastern United States
Clients: Charlotte Area Transit System, Connecticut Department of Transportation, Delaware River Port Authority/PATCO, Massachusetts Bay Transportation Authority, Metropolitan Transportation Authority, MTA Long Island Rail Road, MTA Metro-North Railroad MTA New York City Transit, New Jersey Transit/NJDOT Port Authority Trans-Hudson Corporation, Southeastern Pennsylvania Transportation Authority, The Port Authority of New York & New Jersey
Principal Consultant: LTK Engineering Services, rail systems design, engineering, procurement

Central United States
Clients: Chicago Transit Authority, Dallas Area Rapid Transit, Metropolitan Transit Authority of Harris County, Houston TX, Northern Indiana Commuter Transportation

District, The Metropolitan Council, Minneapolis MN, Trinity Commuter Railway Express
Principal Consultant: LTK Engineering Services, rail systems design, engineering, procurement

Western United States
Clients: California Regional Rail Authority, Denver Regional Transportation District, Los Angeles County Metropolitan Transportation Authority, Sacramento Regional Transit District, San Diego Transit Corporation Sound Transit, Seattle WA, Southern California Regional Rail Authority (SCRRA), The Portland Streetcar, Tri-County Metropolitan Transportation District of Oregon
Principal Consultant: LTK Engineering Services, rail systems design, engineering, procurement

MANUEL PADRON & ASSOCIATES

Atlanta Area Projects
Client: Metropolitan Atlanta Rapid Transit Authority (MARTA), Georgia Regional Transportation Authority (GRTA)
MPA: Bus/rail operation planning, operating cost analysis, financial analysis, technology assessing, alternative evaluating
Principal Consultants: URS Corporation, engineering
PTG, engineering
Parsons Brinckerhoff, engineering

Dallas Area Projects
Client: Dallas Area Rapid Transit (DART)
MPA: Rail/bus operating planning, cost analysis, preliminary engineering
Principal Consultants: URS Corporation, engineering
Carter & Burgess, engineering

Denver Area Projects
Client: Colorado Department of Transportation, Denver Regional Transit District, City of Denver
MPA: Rail/bus operating plans, cost analysis, alternatives analysis, environmental impact statement
Principal Consultants: CH2MHill, engineering, alternatives analysis, environmental impact studies
Carter & Burgess, engineering, highway and transit alternatives analysis, environmental impact statement

Los Angeles Areas Projects
Client: Metropolitan Transit Authority
MPA: Rail/bus operating plans, cost analysis, alternatives analysis, environmental impact statement, project management oversight
Principal Consultants: Korve Engineering, engineering
Parsons Brinckerhoff, engineering, planning
Booze Allen Hamilton, engineering, cost analysis
Gruen Associates, environmental impact statement

San Diego Areas Projects
Client: San Diego Metropolitan Transit System
MPA: Preliminary engineering, environmental impact statement, financial analysis, operating plans
Principal Consultants: Gannett Flemming, engineering
URS Corporation, engineering

San Francisco Bay Area Projects
Client: Bay Area Rapid transit District, San Francisco Municipal Railway, State of California
MPA: Preliminary engineering design, rail operations, financial analysis, operating plans
Principal Consultants: Bechtel, engineering
Parsons Brinckerhoff, engineering
Earth Tech, engineering

Seattle Area Projects
Client: Clients: Sound Transit
MPA: Bus/rail operations planning, financial analysis, contract negotiations
Principal Consultant: Parsons Brinckerhoff, engineering

MOTOR COACH INDUSTRIES, INC.

Coach Models J4500, E4500, D4500
Clients: Georgia Regional Transit Authority, New Jersey Transit, Greyhound Lines, Denver RTD, John Madden E4500 Cruiser, PTRC OmniRide commuter coach

NEW FLYER INDUSTRIES

Hybrid Transit Buses
Clients: King County Metro, Sound Transit, The Bus, Albuquerque Transit Department, Connecticut Transit, etc.
Principal Consultants: New Flyer Industries, design, engineering, manufacture
Caterpillar, diesel engine
Allison, hybrid system
ISE Corporation, gasoline-electric hybrid system

D40i (Invero™)
Clients: Burlington Transit (Burlington, ON); Community Transit (Everett, WA); London Transit Commission (London, ON); OC Transpo (Ottawa, ON); St. Catharines Transit Commission (St. Catharines, ON); Winnipeg Transit (Winnipeg, MB); Roaring Fork Transit Authority, (Aspen, CO)
Principal Consultants: New Flyer, manufacture
New Flyer Research and Development, design, engineering
Cummins, engine
Allison, transmission
Thermo King, HVAC
MAN, axles
USSC, seating

Low-Floor Transit Buses
Clients: Connecticut Transit (Hartford, CT), SEPTA (Philadelphia, PA), Metropolitan Transit Authority (Houston, TX), Capital Metro (Austin, TX), Utah Transit Authority, Salt Lake City, UT), Tri-Met (Portland, OR), Sound Transit (Seattle, WA), King County (Seattle, WA), Omnitrans (San Bernardino, CA), Orange County Transportation Authority (Orange County, CA) and others
Principal Consultants: New Flyer, manufacture
New Flyer Research and Development, design, engineering
Cummins, engine
Allison, transmission
Voith, transmission
ZF, transmission
Thermo King, HVAC
MAN, axles
Meritor, axles
American Seating, seating

NORTH AMERICAN BUS INDUSTRIES INC.—NABI

Model 30-LFN, Shuttle Bus
Clients: Miami-Dade Transit, American Eagle Airlines, Private operators
Principal Consultants: North American Bus Industries Inc.—NABI
Optare Group

Model 35-LFW, 40-LFW, 60-LFW Low-Floor Buses, Model 416, 436 Standard-Floor Buses
Clients: Los Angeles County Metropolitan Transportation Authority, Chicago Transit Authority, Massachusetts Bay Transportation Authority, AC Transit, Foothill Transit, City of Lodi, PACE Suburban Bus, Riverside Transit Agency, Miami-Dade Transit, Regional Transportation District-Denver, Broward County Transit, Southeastern Pennsylvania Transportation Authority and more.
Principal Consultants: North American Bus Industries Inc.—NABI
NABI Rt., engineers and vehicle designer

Model 40C-LFW, 45C-LFW CompoBus® Transit Bus
Clients: City of Phoenix, Los Angeles County Metropolitan Transportation Authority, Chicago Transit Authority, City of Tempe, Antelope Valley Transit Authority
Principal Consultants: North American Bus Industries Inc.—NABI
NABI Rt., engineers and vehicle designer

Model 60-BRT Articulating Bus
Client: Los Angeles County Metropolitan Transportation Authority
Principal Consultants: North American Bus Industries Inc.—NABI
NABI Rt., engineers and vehicle designer

OTAK, INC.

Tacoma LRT
Clients: Sound Transit
Principal Consultants: Otak, project management and controls, civil engineering, street design, drainage design, specifications and estimates, station architecture, urban design, landscape architecture, public art coordination, permitting, public involvement, and construction support services
Architects Rasmussen Triebelhorn
Miller Hull Partnership, station design
Nanda D'Agostino, Sound Transit lead artist, with Nate Slater, Ingrid Lahti, Marianna Hanniger, Nori Sato, and Jerry Mayer
Bruce Dees & Associates, landscape architecture
Carter Burgess, structural engineering
J. Miller & Associates and LTK, lighting
Gary Merlino Construction, general contractor
Haskell Corporation, station fabricator

Tacoma Dome Commuter Rail Station
Clients: Sound Transit
Principal Consultants: Otak, architecture, civil engineering, urban design, public outreach, visualization services
Magnusson Klemencic Associates, structural engineering
Tres West, mechanical and electrical engineering
Nakano Associates, landscape architecture, urban design
EnviroIssues, public outreach
Berschauer Phillips Construction, general contractor

Central Phoenix/East Valley Light Rail Transit
Clients: Valley Metro Rail
Principal Consultants: : Otak in joint venture with Architekton, Norie Sato, Bill Will, station architecture, urban design, artwork

Portland Streetcar
Client: Portland Streetcar, Inc.
Principal Consultants: Otak, civil engineering, environmental planning, public involvement, preliminary and final design, transportation planning
BRW, civil engineering
LTK Engineering Services, operations and maintenance planning, vehicle specifications, electrical and system engineering
Zimmer Gunsul Frasca Partnership, station design
Hong West & Associates, environmental and geotechnical engineering
KJS Associates, traffic analysis

America's Seating.

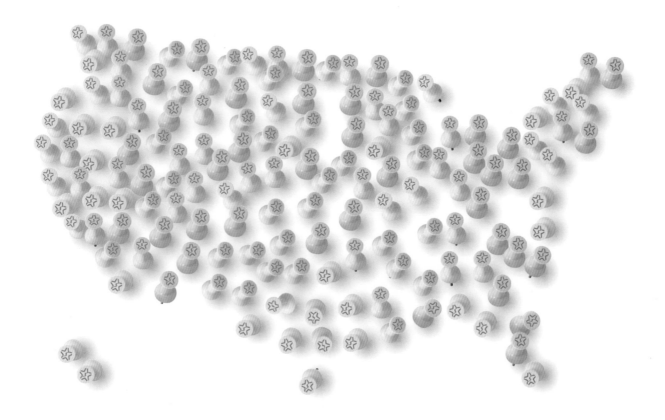

American Seating public transportation seats are in every major city in America.

From California to Maine, we've earned a reputation for quality, innovation and durability. Using state-of-the-art materials and design engineering, American Seating will deliver the highest value and unrivaled passenger comfort. Wherever the road (or rail) may lead, we will strive to exceed customers' expectations.

Call 1-800-748-0268 and discover how American Seating can increase ridership by providing the best in style, comfort and durability.

PARSONS TRANSPORTATION GROUP INC.

WMATA
Client: Washington Metropolitan Area Transit Authority
Principal Consultants: Parsons, General Engineering Consultant

Transportation Expansion Project (T-REX)
Client: Regional Transportation District and Colorado Department of Transportation
Principal Consultants: Parsons, joint venture design management
Parsons Transportation Group, Inc., in joint venture with Peter Kiewit & Sons (prime contractor)
Kiewit Construction, joint venture construction management

MBTA Operations Control Center
Client: Massachusetts Bay Transportation Authority (MBTA)
Principal Consultants: Parsons, design, installation management

Charlotte South Corridor Light Rail Project
Client: Charlotte Area Transit System
Principal Consultants: Parsons, prime consultant

RNL DESIGN

Foothill Transit Operations & Maintenance Facility
Client: Foothill Transit
Principal Consultants: RNL Design, master planning, architecture, interior design
Maintenance Design Group, maintenance consultant, programming
Martin & Huang International, structural engineer
Storms & Low, mechanical, electrical, plumbing engineer
Delon Hampton & Associates, civil engineer
Melandrez Associates, landscape architect
Golder Associates, geotechnical engineer
Jacobus & Yuang, cost estimator
Orbcom, communications specialist
Kumar Consultant Services, project management
EQE International, construction manager
AMEC, testing and inspection
APSI, project controls

RTD-LRT Elati Maintenance Facility
Client: Regional Transportation District (RTD)
Principal Consultants: RNL Design, architecture, interior design, design management and coordination
Maintenance Design Group, project management, programming, maintenance equipment, construction engineering & inspection
Carter & Burgess, structural, mechanical, electrical, plumbing, fire protection engineering
Milestone Engineering, civil engineering
Land Mark Design, landscape architecture
Hanscomb, cost estimating
Booz, Allen, Hamilton, track and OCS coordination
Roof Tech, roofing consultant
Kumar, geotechnical engineer
M.A. Mortenson, general contractor

Old Town Transit Center
Client: Park City Corporation
Principal Consultants: RNL Design, programming, urban design, site planning, architectural design
Cooper Roberts Simonsen Architects, architect of record
LSC Transportation Consultants, transportation planning
Sear-Brown, civil engineer
Thomas Engineering, structural and mechanical engineering
Black McCutchen, landscape architecture
Agra Earth and Environment, environmental consultant
Construction Control Corporation, cost estimating
Herm Hughes & Son, Inc., general contractor

Mesa Transit Maintenance & Operations Facility
Client: City of Mesa
Principal Consultants: RNL Design, master planning, architecture, interior design
Maintenance Design Group, maintenance consultant, programming,
GLHN, mechanical, electrical engineer
Paul Koehler Engineering, structural engineer
Morea-Hall, civil engineer
Logan Simpson Design, landscape architecture
Associated Construction Economists, cost estimator
Fuel Solutions, fueling consultant
Speedie & Associates, geotechnical engineering
Stantec, construction project manager
D.L. Withers, general contractor

SASAKI ASSOCIATES, INC.

Dallas Area Rapid Transit Mall
Client: Dallas Area Rapid Transit Authority
Principal Consultants: Sasaki Associates, landscape architecture, urban design, project management
Campos Engineers, electrical engineering
Berryhill-Loyd, structural engineering
Arrendondo & Brunz; Huitt-Zollars, civil engineering
Branston Partnership, lighting engineering
HJM, architecture
Oglesby Greene, architecture
Brad Goldberg, artist

San Francisco Waterfront Transportation Projects
Client: City and County of San Francisco
Principal Consultants: Sasaki Associates, urban design, planning, landscape architecture
Levy Design Partners, architecture
AGS, civil engineering
Cambridge Systematics, traffic engineering
Anna Valentina Murch, artist (N-Line shelters)
Helene Fried Associates, cultural resources
Tom Keilani Design Associates, graphics, environmental signage

Cleveland Waterfront Transit Line
Client: Greater Cleveland Regional Transit Authority
Principal Consultants: Sasaki Associates, urban design, planning, landscape architecture, traffic engineering, graphic design
Parsons Brinckerhoff, prime consultant
Robert P. Madison International, architecture

Euclid Avenue Bus Rapid Transit Corridor
Client: Greater Cleveland Regional Transit Authority
Principal Consultants: Sasaki Associates, urban design, landscape architecture, graphic design
Wilbur Smith Associates, prime consultant
The Outside In, landscape architecture
Whelan Communications, public relations
Robert P. Madison International, architecture
Finkbeiner, Pettis & Strout, civil engineering
Kapp and Associates, graphics

SIEMENS TRANSPORTATION SYSTEMS, INC.

New York City Transit Rail Automation
Client: Metropolitan Transit Authority-New York City Transit
Principal Consultants: Siemens, joint venture leader, operation control systems, automatic train control systems, telecommunication systems
Railworks Comstock, installation
Union Switch & Signal, conventional signaling
E.A.Technologies/Petrocelli joint venture, installation

MAX Light Rail Vehicles and Electrification
Client: Tri-County Metropolitan Transportation District (TriMet)
Principal Consultants: Siemens, light rail vehicles, power substation, overhead catenary, signaling and telecommunications
LTK Engineering Services, vehicles
Stacy and Witbeck, consortium leader, construction management (Interstate MAX)
Elcon, systems coordinator (Westside Extension)

METRORail
Client: Metropolitan Transit Authority of Harris County
Principal Consultants: Siemens, light rail vehicles, communications, supervisory control and data acquisition (SCADA), signaling, ticket vending, civil work, track work, and traction power supply, traction power distribution, overhead catenary
LTK Engineering Services, vehicles
STV, design and build

SILVESTER+TAFURO, INC.

Retail Shops in Terminals
Client: d-parture spa
Principal Consultants: Silvester+Tafuro, Inc., space planning, design development, contract administration
N.H. Fedder Associates, lighting design
John J. Guth Engineering P.C., consulting engineers, MEP engineers
STSC Consulting Group, Inc., architecture
Salon Interiors, commercial cabinetry

Retail Shops in Train Stations
Clients: The Hudson Group
Principal Consultants: Silvester+Tafuro, Inc., interior design
STSC Consulting Group, Inc., architecture
Susan Brady Lighting Design, Inc., lighting design
FMC Associates, MEP engineers
Tally Display, media consulting

Amtrak Auto Train Superliner Conversion
Clients: Amtrak
Principal Consultants: Silvester+Tafuro, Inc., space planning, design development, contract documents, materials specification, fabrication supervision

Retail Shops in Terminals
Clients: Passport Travel Spa–Indianapolis International Airport
Principal Consultants: Silvester+Tafuro, Inc., site selection, branding, contract documents, design implementation, project managers and airport designers
STSC Consulting Group, Inc., architecture
Mussett, Nicholas & Associated, MEP engineers
Habitech Corporation of America, interior design

Safety Vision

Mobile Video Surveillance Solutions
Houston, Texas

By road and by rail, our camera systems are reducing risk, increasing profitability, preventing accidents, and saving lives. Business doesn't get more important than that.

For over a decade, Safety Vision has helped you safeguard valuable commodities—your drivers, your passengers, and your property. Founded in 1993, we honed our expertise in mobile rear-vision camera systems before expanding into the mobile video recording market. Today, we are a leading provider of onboard surveillance and mobile camera systems for transit, light-rail, and pupil transportation authorities and fleets.

Over the years, we have evolved from a distributor to the *designer, manufacturer, and installer* of our own suite of products. Product innovations include our SideVision™ cameras; our compact LCD monitor with built-in control box; and our RoadRecorder® digital video recorder series. This series is composed of several models, specially designed to support different market segments. Technology innovations include SafetyNet™, a wireless bus-yard data collection network solution.

We're supporting you in new markets, as well. Our 2005 entrance into the police video market expanded our presence in the public safety/emergency response sector. Our strength in that sector, coupled with strategic partnerships, positions us to support government-funded emergency preparedness and interagency communications interoperability efforts—e.g., the DHS-sponsored first responder initiative.

True communications interoperability requires cross-platform compatibility. Our RoadRecorder series is an integral component of the industry-leading solution to the wireless communication and long-term management of video, voice, and data files. Today, we are a *total solution provider*, offering you a comprehensive yet streamlined answer to your mobile video surveillance needs.◉

Above: Artist's rendering of Safety Vision's new corporate headquarters in Houston. Our move to new ground was prompted by our phenomenal growth: In 2004 alone, our staff grew nearly two-fold to accommodate our steadily escalating sales volume. Our new 7-acre campus combines expanded office and research & development space with a four-tier, high-storage logistics warehouse. Now more than ever, we are able to respond to your needs quickly, efficiently—*cost effectively.*

Above: Safety Vision's QuickView™ module connected to a PC viewing station running our SafetyView® video viewing software: The module houses the system's removable hard drive canister, which contains video recorded in transit.

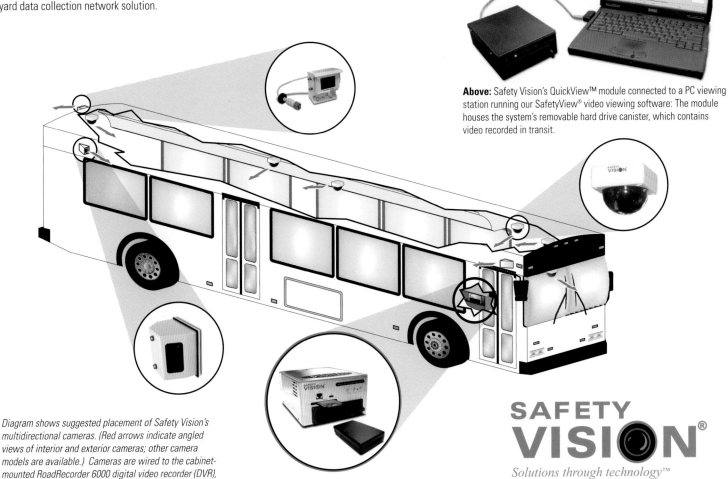

Diagram shows suggested placement of Safety Vision's multidirectional cameras. (Red arrows indicate angled views of interior and exterior cameras; other camera models are available.) Cameras are wired to the cabinet-mounted RoadRecorder 6000 digital video recorder (DVR), which offers up to 10-camera capability. Currently installed and operating on several thousand transit and other vehicles nationwide, the RoadRecorder series now includes the RailRecorder™ DVR, tailored to the railed transit market.

Above: Safety Vision's RoadRecorder 6000 digital video recorder and removable hard drive canister: The canister contains encrypted video that may serve as a training aid or as court-admissable evidence.

SAFETY VISION®
Solutions through technology™

800.880.8855
email@safetyvision.com

Retail Shops in Terminals
Clients: Tread 2
Principal Consultants: Silvester+Tafuro, Inc., space planning, interior design, design development, project management
John J. Guth Engineering P.C., consulting engineers, MEP engineers
STSC Consulting Group, Inc., architecture

STACY AND WITBECK, INC.

Interstate Max Light Right Line Extension
Clients: Tri-County Metropolitan Transportation District of Oregon (Tri-Met)
Principal Consultants: Stacy and Witbeck, general contractor
Pinnell Busch, pre-construction phase
PB Civil Design Team/ZGF Zimmer Gunsul Frasca Partnership, lead architect
PB Civil Design Team/BRW A Division of URS Corporation/OTAK, lead engineer
Northeast Urban, Dirt & Aggregate Interchange, Capital, Hamilton, Tice, K&M, Workhorse, Whitaker Ellis, Green Art, Ilsand, JEC, CEC, FMB, AGB, Suell Ampere, major subcontractors

Mid-Embarcadero Surface Roadway and F-Line Extension
Clients: San Francisco Department of Public Works
Principal Consultant: Stacy and Witbeck, general contractor

University and Medical Center Light Rail Transit Lines
Clients: Utah Transit Authority
Principal Consultants: SLC Rail Constructors, joint venture team: Stacy and Witbeck, Flatiron Structures, Geneva Rock Products
CHS Designers, joint venture team: CH2M Hill, Hatch Mott MacDonald, STV, engineering and design
Mass Electric Construction Company, overhead contact system
Gerber Construction, structures
Cache Valley Electric, electrical and traffic signals
Parsons-Brinckerhoff, program manager
Carter-Burgess, construction manager

SUMITOMO CORPORATION OF AMERICA

Commuter Rail
Clients: Chicago Metropolitan Rail (Metra), Maryland Transit Administration (MARC)
Principal Consultants: Sumitomo Corporation of America, prime contractor
Nippon Sharyo, car building partner

Gallery-Type Bi-Level Commuter Rail Push-Pull Passenger Car
Clients: Chicago Metropolitan Rail (Metra), State of California Department of Transportation (Caltrain)
Principal Consultants: Sumitomo Corporation of America, prime contractor
Nippon Sharyo, car building partner

Articulated Light Rail Vehicle
Client: Los Angeles County MTA
Principal Consultants: Sumitomo Corporation of America, prime contractor
Nippon Sharyo, car building partner

Crystal Mover Automated People Mover System
Clients: Metropolitan Washington Airports Authority; American Airlines/Miami-Dade Aviation Department
Principal Consultants: Sumitomo Corporation, prime contractor for the supply of the system and operations and maintenance
Mitsubishi Heavy Industries, LTD., system integrator and supplier, vehicle manufacturer
Alcatel Transport Automation Solutions, automatic train control supplier

YOU DON'T HAVE TO RIDE PUBLIC TRANSPORTATION TO BENEFIT FROM IT.

Every day more than 14 million Americans use safe, reliable and convenient public transportation services. But all Americans — whether they live in cities, suburbs or rural areas — benefit from public transportation, even if they never board a train or bus.

Our public transportation infrastructure needs to keep pace with the growing demand and continue to provide the personal, economic, energy and environmental benefits that improve all our lives. Public transportation promotes a healthy economy and creates jobs for millions of citizens. To learn more, visit www.publictransportation.org.

PUBLIC TRANSPORTATION
Wherever life takes you

APTA
AMERICAN
PUBLIC
TRANSPORTATION
ASSOCIATION

Index by Project / Vehicle

The Designer Series

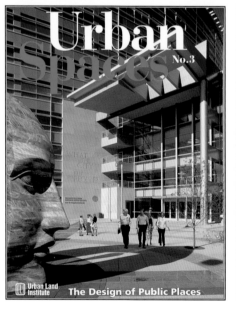

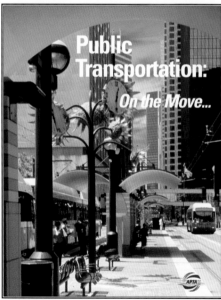

Visual Reference Publications, Inc.

302 Fifth Avenue, New York, NY 10001

Tel: 212.279.7000 • Fax: 212.279.7014

www.visualreference.com

Acknowledgments

Thanks to all the great people at the APTA whose support and cooperation made this book possible, especially William Millar, Rose Sheridan and Karen Doyle.

The combined editorial expertise and knowledge of architecture and the elements of design of Marc Wortman, our editor, and John Dixon, our consulting editor, was essential to the task of successfully presenting and writing about the over 150 projects and vehicles showcased in *Public Transportation: On the Move.*

Harish Patel's graphic design and layouts, and most importantly, his ability to communicate with the designers and representatives of the participating firms made the copy flow smoothly and resulted in the production of a visually attractive and exciting book.

The design and production professionals involved in dealing with the many details of the publishing process were responsible for the timely schedules and high quality production that was achieved. Thanks to Amy Yip and John Hogan at VRP and Avan Lee and Fanny Huang at our printers.

The architects, designers, marketing directors and coordinators, and all the personnel of the firms with whom we worked were terrific. Through our numerous conversations, I made many friends and their responsiveness and enthusiasm made publishing *Public Transportation* a most enjoyable experience from concept through creation.

Henry Burr
Publisher

Thanks to the following advertisers for their support: